T0328473

Cambridge Elements ≡

Elements in England in the Early Medieval World
edited by
Megan Cavell
University of Birmingham
Rory Naismith
University of Cambridge
Winfried Rudolf
University of Göttingen
Emily V. Thornbury
Yale University

EUROPE AND
THE ANGLO-SAXONS

Francesca Tinti

Universidad del País Vasco UPV/EHU
IKERBASQUE, Basque Foundation for Science

CAMBRIDGE
UNIVERSITY PRESS

CAMBRIDGE
UNIVERSITY PRESS

University Printing House, Cambridge CB2 8BS, United Kingdom

One Liberty Plaza, 20th Floor, New York, NY 10006, USA

477 Williamstown Road, Port Melbourne, VIC 3207, Australia

314–321, 3rd Floor, Plot 3, Splendor Forum, Jasola District Centre, New Delhi – 110025, India

103 Penang Road, #05–06/07, Visioncrest Commercial, Singapore 238467

Cambridge University Press is part of the University of Cambridge.

It furthers the University's mission by disseminating knowledge in the pursuit of education, learning, and research at the highest international levels of excellence.

www.cambridge.org
Information on this title: www.cambridge.org/9781108931953
DOI: 10.1017/9781108942898

© Francesca Tinti 2021

First published 2021

A catalogue record for this publication is available from the British Library.

ISBN 978-1-108-93195-3 Paperback
ISSN 2632-203X (online)
ISSN 2632-2021 (print)

Cambridge University Press has no responsibility for the persistence or accuracy of URLs for external or third-party internet websites referred to in this publication and does not guarantee that any content on such websites is, or will remain, accurate or appropriate.

Europe and the Anglo-Saxons

Elements in England in the Early Medieval World

DOI: 10.1017/9781108942898
First published online: July 2021

Francesca Tinti
Universidad del País Vasco UPV/EHU

IKERBASQUE, Basque Foundation for Science

Author for correspondence: Francesca Tinti, francesca.tinti@ehu.eus

Abstract: This publication explores the interactions between the inhabitants of early medieval England and their contemporaries in continental Europe. Starting with a brief excursus on previous treatments of the topic, the discussion then focuses on Anglo-Saxon geographical perceptions and representations of Europe and of Britain's place in it, before moving on to explore relations with Rome, dynasties and diplomacy, religious missions and monasticism, travel, trade and warfare. This Element demonstrates that the Anglo-Saxons' relations with the continent had a major impact on the shaping of their political, economic, religious and cultural life.

Keywords: Europe, Anglo-Saxon, early medieval, travel, connections

ISBNs: 9781108931953 (PB), 9781108942898 (OC)
ISSNs: 2632-203X (online), 2632-2021 (print)

Contents

1 Introduction

Interactions between the inhabitants of early medieval England and their contemporaries in continental Europe were numerous, varied and influential. In recent decades several studies have explored different aspects of these relations, often challenging older approaches that had tended to convey a general sense of marked separation between England and the rest of the European continent.[1] Migrations, missionary activities, correspondence, diplomacy, travel, wars, conquests and other forms of direct contact have been investigated in order to understand their scope and significance. *Europe and the Anglo-Saxons* aims to provide a guide to these contacts, while paying special attention to issues of identities, perceptions and representations.[2] In other words, this Element will not just consider what the Anglo-Saxons and the inhabitants of continental Europe did with each other, but also what they thought of each other. As will become apparent below, this topic has traditionally been framed as one concerning 'England and the continent', whereas the order of the two elements has been deliberately inverted here and their connotations modified through the employment of different terminology. Both 'Europe' and 'Anglo-Saxons' are topical and, in some senses, problematic terms; both are attested – through corresponding Latin and/or vernacular words – in written sources from our period; and both are characterized in Modern English discourse by a range of semantic connotations, which become even more varied when one takes into account the meanings and nuances of corresponding terms in other modern languages (e.g. French *anglo-saxon*, Italian *anglosassone*, German *angelsächsisch*). For these reasons it is necessary to clarify at the outset the rationale behind these terminological choices.

The word *Europa* mostly occurs in early medieval Latin texts to indicate one of the three parts of the known world: Asia, Europe and Africa. Occasionally the same term is used to refer more specifically to the Christian territories north of the Mediterranean, as is the case in two letters which the Irish missionary Columbanus sent in the late sixth and early seventh centuries to Popes Gregory the Great and Boniface IV respectively.[3] Later on, in the Carolingian period, the term was employed in connection with Charlemagne's rule and military conquests; for instance, in *c.*775, the Englishman Cathwulf, in a letter addressed to the king, wrote that God had raised him 'in honorem glorie regni Europe' ('to the honour of the glory of the kingdom of Europe'), whereas

---

[1] See, on this point, Nelson, 'England and the Continent in the Ninth Century', 10–15.

[2] This publication will focus on mainland Europe, while relations between England and the rest of the insular world will be considered in another Element of this Cambridge series.

[3] Gundlach, ed., *Columbae sive Columbani epistolae*, nos. 1, 5, pp. 156, 170.

Alcuin in a letter of 790 commented on the expansion of the church in Europe through reference to the conversion of the Saxons and the Frisians, which was achieved 'instante rege Karolo', that is, through Charlemagne's urging.[4] In recent decades, however, a number of scholars have observed that occurrences of the term in surviving sources are not particularly numerous and that in medieval writings it is not possible to appreciate a 'tangible reality' for Europe as more than a straightforwardly geographical concept.[5] In these scholars' view, Europe does not seem to have played a particularly meaningful role in the construction of its inhabitants' identities, and historians should be wary of the dangers of back-projecting modern preoccupations onto early medieval sources.[6] Interestingly, it has also been noted that in the early medieval period Europe was mentioned most frequently in texts written by insular, especially Anglo-Saxon scholars, such as those mentioned above.[7] This has been tentatively explained as a possibly '"eccentric" perspective onto the realms of the Continent' due to an eagerness to convey 'a generalizing notion of Europe'.[8] Authors from the edges of Europe, that is, Britain and Ireland, would seem to have aspired to being integrated into a larger whole, which could no longer be achieved through ancient models, and the Carolingian emperor's successes would appear to have provided the best approximation available in the West.[9] Whether the insular perspective was really that 'eccentric' remains to be ascertained, but these observations highlight the need for further investigation into the ways in which Europe was perceived and described by learned Anglo-Saxons. As will emerge below in Section 3, the available evidence indicates that geographical descriptions of 'Europe' produced in early medieval England could differ in significant details, revealing evolving perceptions about Britain's location and its relations with the European continent.[10]

---

[4] Dümmler, ed., *Epistolae variorum Carolo Magno regnante scriptae*, no. 7, p. 503; Dümmler, ed., *Alcuini sive Albini epistolae*, no. 7, p. 32.

[5] Oschema, 'Medieval Europe', 59.

[6] This position, mostly held by German scholars, can be contrasted with the enthusiasm with which several French (and other) historians in the last decades of the twentieth century drew frequent parallels between Carolingian Europe and the nascent European Union: Isaïa, 'L'empire carolingien'. On modern historians' shifting perceptions of such parallels see also Nelson, 'Charlemagne and Europe', and West, 'Plenty of Puff'.

[7] Oschema, 'Medieval Europe', 60; Nelson, 'Charlemagne and Europe', 130.

[8] Oschema, 'Medieval Europe', 60.

[9] Schneidmüller, 'Die mittelalterlichen Konstruktionen', 10; Nelson, 'Charlemagne and Europe', 130.

[10] Readers should bear in mind that while Britain, that is, the island as a geographical concept, was commonly referred to in early medieval sources, 'England' (or *Englalond* in Old English) only made its appearance fairly late in our period. Its employment in academic publications on the early Middle Ages must therefore be understood as a shorthand for the territories where the Anglo-Saxons lived rather than presumed to provide any sense of collective identification with a 'nation'.

As has traditionally been done in historical and archaeological studies, 'Anglo-Saxons' is employed in this Element as a convenient label to refer to the people who inhabited the territory roughly corresponding to modern England in the early medieval period; that is, from the settlement, in the fifth and sixth centuries, of continental Germanic-speaking migrants from central and northern Europe until the Norman Conquest of 1066.[11] However, given the length of the period and the range of political, military, social and cultural developments which it witnessed, it is important to recognize that behind the unifying ethnonym 'Anglo-Saxons' there were in fact people who lived under notably diverse circumstances.

Other, more problematic issues concerning the employment of this term have emerged in recent years in connection with modern, racially charged uses of the adjective 'Anglo-Saxon'. This has led to intense debate as to whether the ethnonym should be abandoned altogether in scholarly publications dealing with early medieval England.[12] Several participants in the debate have observed that the term (or, rather, Latin versions of it) was first employed in early medieval sources written in continental Europe. The earliest occurrence can be found in the late eighth-century *Historia Langobardorum* by Paul the Deacon, in a passage comparing the way in which early Lombards dressed with the garments worn by the *Anglisaxones* of Paul's time. A few decades later, the author of the anonymous *Vita Alcuini*, most likely dating to the 820s, employed the word *Engelsaxo* to refer to an English priest named Aigulf, who had visited Alcuin at Tours.[13] In the tenth century Widukind of Corvey explained the origin of the ethnonym *Anglisaxones* – which he explicitly says was used in his time – as relating to their inhabiting an island located in a corner ('in angulo') of the sea.[14] Although the use of the term within modern scholarship owes more to its sixteenth-century resurrection than to any conscious reference to its much older continental origins,[15] 'Anglo-Saxons' is employed

---

[11] Incidentally, it should be noted that neither of these two events, nor their immediate aftermath, will be treated in much detail in this Element; their inherent 'European connections' should in any case be self-evident.

[12] For a balanced résumé and discussion see Wood, 'Is It Time'. For an older, but in many respects still pertinent, analysis of some of the issues raised by the employment of the term 'Anglo-Saxon', see Reynolds, 'What Do We Mean'. See also, more recently, Rambaran-Olm, 'Misnaming the Medieval' and Wilton, 'What Do We Mean'.

[13] Bethmann and Waitz, eds., *Pauli Historia Langobardorum*, IV.22, p. 124; Foulke, trans., *Paul the Deacon: History of the Lombards*, 166. Arndt, ed., *Vita Alcuini*, c. 18, p. 193. For further examples and for the suggestion that the label was created to distinguish the 'Anglian' Saxons from the continental Saxons, see Levison, *England and the Continent*, 92–3, n. 1.

[14] Hirsch and Lohmann, eds., *Die Sachsengeschichte des Widukind von Korvei*, I.8, p. 10 ('quia illa insula in angulo quodam maris sita est, Anglisaxones usque hodie vocitantur').

[15] On the creation of the notion of 'Anglo-Saxon England' in Tudor times, see Niles, *The Idea of Anglo-Saxon England*, 49–76.

in this Element on the relations between England and continental Europe to acknowledge the significance of those very origins and in light of the fundamental role played by 'others', that is those who are perceived as external to a specific group, in the creation of ethnic identities.[16]

Of course, 'Anglo-Saxons' is not the only ethnonym appearing in this Element to refer to the inhabitants of early medieval England, as either for stylistic reasons or in order to reflect more closely the specific terminology employed in different sources, other descriptors also occur. 'English' or 'early English' appear as well, but it should be borne in mind that the use of 'English' as an ethnic label is not without problems either, as it risks drawing direct, unwarranted connections with the modern English nation. In fact, in the UK 'English' and 'England' feature more prominently in extremist language than 'Anglo-Saxon' does, with the latter being associated in common parlance with England's early medieval past.[17] In other words, this is a complex, evolving and multifaceted matter, raising different issues in different countries. Readers should be aware of the ongoing debates and, more generally, of the limitations and inevitable shortcomings of several of the ethnonyms employed in modern scholarship to refer to early medieval societies.

Europe and the Anglo-Saxons explores how the Anglo-Saxons perceived and described their relations with and location in Europe, and, conversely, the ways in which their contemporaries on the continent represented and referred to them. The discussion will focus on six main themes, starting with Anglo-Saxon geographical perceptions and representations of Europe (Section 3), followed by relations with Rome and the papacy (Section 4), then courts, diplomacy and dynasties (Section 5), religious missions and monasticism (Section 6), travel and trade (Section 7) and, finally, warfare and conquests (Section 8). A timeline is also provided to help readers locate the main events and people mentioned. Before moving on to the core themes, however, it is necessary to present a brief excursus on previous treatments of this topic (Section 2) so as to situate the present work within the historiographical tradition, and acknowledge the role played by contemporary political, cultural and economic preoccupations in shaping our approach to the study of the (early medieval) past.

2 Precedents

Modern studies of the relations between early medieval England and continental Europe are all at least in part indebted to the pioneering work of Wilhelm

---

[16] Pohl, 'Ethnic Names and Identities', 10; Geary, 'Ethnic Identity'. This is obviously not to say that the people living in early medieval England were invariably called 'Anglo-Saxons' by their contemporaries on the continent, as uses shifted with time and space.

[17] See Naismith, *Early Medieval Britain*, 114–15.

Levison and, more specifically, his volume of 1946, which gathers the Ford Lectures he delivered at Oxford three years earlier. Levison's focus was on the eighth century, which he described as a period of major English 'contribution to the spiritual foundations and unity of Western civilization'.[18] Behind a language that twenty-first-century readers will find outdated, there was the personal experience of a Jewish scholar who had fled Nazi Germany in 1939 and had been able to find a new home in England after taking up an invitation from the University of Durham.[19] In Levison's book the comparison between the work of eighth-century Anglo-Saxon missionaries in pagan Germanic-speaking continental regions and the role played by England in the author's own time is explicit: both then and in his own times he could see 'a broad, deep, and lasting influence upon continental ways of thought and life'.[20] Among the many lessons that Levison's work offers us in exploring the relations between England and the continent in the early Middle Ages, one should include the role that every scholar's personal circumstances play in the shaping of their work. This is of course a truism, but one worth mentioning in a publication written in the aftermath of the Brexit referendum, at a time when debates on the meaning and role of Europe as both a geographical and political entity – and the place of Britain and England in it – inevitably affect current perceptions of England in early medieval Europe.[21]

As Conrad Leyser has noted, it would take some time for the significance of Levison's work to be recognized in Britain; among the main reasons for this late reception, Leyser mentions the hesitant state of the relations between Britain and Germany in the aftermath of the Second World War and the dominating role that France played within the continental horizons of medieval research culture in Britain at that time.[22] In his view, German scholars were quicker to acknowledge the importance of Levison's findings, especially with reference to the moral authority that the eighth-century Anglo-Saxon missionaries – above all, Boniface – provided for the Carolingians' political and military expansion.[23] It is important to remember, however, that an interest in all things Anglo-Saxon had been prominent in German scholarship from much earlier on, as is made evident by the development of philological studies in the context of rising German nationalism. The Germanic dialects of early English vernacular texts

---

[18] Levison, *England and the Continent*, 1.
[19] For a detailed analysis of the ways in which Levison's work was conditioned by his personal circumstances, see Leyser, 'Introduction', 2–3.
[20] Levison, *England and the Continent*, 1.
[21] Several medieval historians have taken an active role in such debates, either to advocate Britain's differences and separation from Europe (e.g. Abulafia, 'Britain'), or to demonstrate pre-Conquest England's unambiguous involvement with the continent (e.g. West, 'England').
[22] Leyser, 'Introduction', 5.   [23] As exemplified by Schieffer, *Winfrid-Bonifatius*.

allowed late eighteenth- and early nineteenth-century scholars to consider the Anglo-Saxons one of the 'German' peoples, thus providing the intellectual milieu and the institutional support for the production of works such as Felix Liebermann's masterpiece edition of Anglo-Saxon law codes.[24]

Back in Britain, renewed efforts towards early medieval research encompassing both England and the continent can be found in the work of the Oxford scholar Michael Wallace-Hadrill. Interestingly, his first publications on these topics were more about comparisons than contacts and, just as Conrad Leyser has observed, they leaned especially towards Francophone regions.[25] This would change later on, both thanks to the adoption of a wider geographical framework and through deliberate efforts to explore connections between England and the continent.[26] Work in these areas became more widespread and less dependent on specific individual initiatives in the 1970s and 1980s, also as a consequence of the United Kingdom joining the European Economic Community in 1973. The insularity which had characterized many of the earlier studies of Anglo-Saxon England thus began to be superseded in publications from that period.[27] Later on, wider collective initiatives, such as the Transformation of the Roman World programme, funded by the European Science Foundation in the 1990s, played a major role in making European early medievalists think beyond the traditional frameworks of their respective national histories, thus also placing early English history more firmly in a European context. Also dating from this time is a volume edited by Nigel Saul – entitled *England in Europe* – which focuses on the later Middle Ages but includes an initial chapter by Janet L. Nelson on the Anglo-Saxon period; here the author provides a brief but incisive overview on the many types of relations that linked England with continental Europe, paying special attention to the increasingly complex political, diplomatic and religious contacts of the tenth and first half of the eleventh centuries. Late Anglo-Saxon England is depicted as a profoundly European polity, whose history would be 'incomprehensible without its continental context'.[28]

---

[24] Liebermann, ed., *Die Gesetze der Angelsachsen*. See Fruscione, 'Liebermann's Intellectual Milieu', 20–1 and Rabin, 'Felix Liebermann', 4.

[25] See for example Wallace-Hadrill, 'The Franks and the English'; Wallace-Hadrill, 'Rome and the Early English Church'.

[26] For example, see Wallace-Hadrill, *Bede's Europe*; Wallace-Hadrill, *Early Germanic Kingship*. For a detailed discussion of Wallace-Hadrill's life and work, see Wood, 'John Michael Wallace-Hadrill'.

[27] See for instance Campbell, ed., *The Anglo-Saxons*, 61–7, 118–22, 170–1.

[28] Nelson, 'England and the Continent in the Anglo-Saxon Period', 35. A specific interest in the late Anglo-Saxon period also features in Ortenberg, *The English Church*, though the attention in this case focuses on artistic connections with the continent.

Similar standpoints can be observed in the production of major collaborative publications which appeared in the same period, such as the two volumes of the New Cambridge Medieval History which cover the early Middle Ages. In Volume 2, published in 1995 and dealing with the eighth and ninth centuries, the editor – Rosamond McKitterick – chose to open this collection of essays with an initial section on the British Isles, which ended with a chapter on 'England and the Continent' that she authored herself.[29] Perhaps even more interestingly, Volume 3, which appeared in the year 2000 and was edited by the late Timothy Reuter, includes England in a section on post-Carolingian Europe.[30] Such efforts became even more explicit in the four presidential addresses that Janet L. Nelson delivered between 2001 and 2004, during her tenure as the first female President of the Royal Historical Society. Her chosen topic – of explicit Levisonian inspiration – was 'England and the Continent in the Ninth Century'. Although, as she declared in her first address, it is 'less easy to write a story of Anglo-Continental connections in the ninth century than for the eighth century',[31] Nelson provided a magisterial example of how that can and should be done, offering insightful discussion of several instances of such contacts, as well as elegant comparative analysis of major themes in ninth-century English and continental history. Similarly, in a monograph published in 2003,[32] Joanna Story took over from where Levison had left his account of the English contribution to continental history, that is, at the end of the eighth century, when – he noted – the direction of 'the current ... reversed',[33] as the continent began to exert increasing influence on the Anglo-Saxon kingdoms. Story covered the period up to 870, not only showing the variety of cross-Channel relations in the late eighth and ninth centuries, but also providing several examples of the deep influence that Carolingian Francia had on contemporary England, not least in providing models for Anglo-Saxon kingship.

The nature and extent of Carolingian influence on the political, cultural and ecclesiastical history of early medieval England have been at the centre of numerous other publications. A number of authors have argued, for instance, that Carolingian texts were the main sources of inspiration for the late Anglo-Saxon church in general, and the tenth-century monastic reform in particular.[34] However, although late Anglo-Saxon England is often described as finally 'catching up' with the continent thanks to the arrival of texts and ideas associated with earlier reforming efforts in the Carolingian Empire, from other angles

---

[29] McKitterick, 'England and the Continent'.   [30] Keynes, 'England, c.900–1016'.

[31] Nelson, 'England and the Continent in the Ninth Century', 3.

[32] Story, *Carolingian Connections*.   [33] Levison, *England and the Continent*, 107.

[34] See, for example, Jones, 'The Book of the Liturgy' and bibliography cited there. See also below, Section 6.

the English church has been described as anticipating practices which were subsequently adopted elsewhere. One example is the translation of bishops, which was fairly common in the late Anglo-Saxon period, when kings translated to Canterbury bishops who already held West Saxon episcopal sees, but became more frequent across western Christendom in the twelfth century.[35] Ecclesiastical politics and, more specifically, the roles of bishops in the pre-Gregorian period have provided especially fertile ground for comparative analyses of late Anglo-Saxon England and Ottonian-Salian Germany,[36] building on the foundational work of scholars like Karl Leyser and Timothy Reuter.[37] Such recent initiatives stand out for bringing together British and German scholars, though it is certainly still the case that continental early medieval historians rarely 'cross the Channel' to include Britain in their investigations. Over the years, there have been, of course, several other exceptions, but it must be acknowledged that in spite of the efforts made in recent decades to overcome old separations, national historiographical traditions still loom large behind both scholars' choices and research funding policies.

3 Geographical Perceptions and Representations

> Britain, once called Albion, is an island of the ocean and lies to the north-west, being opposite Germany, Gaul, and Spain, which form the greater part of Europe, though at a considerable distance from them.[38]

These are the words with which Bede chose to open the first chapter of his *Historia ecclesiastica gentis Anglorum*, in a passage which is closely modelled on the description of Britain that Pliny made in his *Naturalis Historia*, with some detail also provided by Orosius' early fifth-century *Historiae adversus paganos*. Bede's adoption of ancient geographical perspectives, which oriented the earth from the position of Rome, is highly indicative of the way in which eighth-century learned Anglo-Saxons perceived their place in the world. Rome remained the centre while they were undoubtedly at the periphery, or even the edges of the known world. Yet, as has been demonstrated by Andy Merrills, Bede's adoption of such ancient perspectives was not entirely passive, but served what the author probably perceived as higher, more important aims: by showing that Christianity had reached the edges of the world, he assigned

---

[35] Tinti, 'The Archiepiscopal Pallium', 313; Pennington, *Popes and Bishops*, 85–100.

[36] Körntgen and Waßenhoven, eds., *Patterns of Episcopal Power*; Körntgen and Waßenhoven, eds., *Religion and Politics in the Middle Ages*.

[37] Leyser, 'The Ottonians and Wessex'; Reuter, 'The Making of England and Germany'.

[38] Colgrave and Mynors, eds. and trans., *Bede's Ecclesiastical History*, I.1, pp. 14–15 ('Brittania Oceani insula, cui quondam Albion nomen fuit, inter septentrionem et occidentem locata est, Germaniae Galliae Hispaniae, maximis Europae partibus, multo interuallo aduersa').

Britain a special place in divine history.[39] This opening geographical section of the first chapter of the *Historia ecclesiastica* draws on a number of different sources, including, as well as Pliny and Orosius, Gildas and Solinus. The passage quoted above is followed by a description of Britain's size, with details of its length and width (taken from Gildas) and the extent of the whole circuit of its coastline (derived from Solinus). Bede then looks south again, towards the continent and, following Orosius, states that *Gallia Belgica* lies to the south of Britain and that for those crossing the sea to reach the island from there, the closest port was *Rutubi portus*, as indeed Orosius had called this place, though Bede is also quick to add that it was now called *Reptacaestir* (i.e. modern Richborough) by the English. Then, borrowing again from Pliny, he says that fifty miles across from this port lay *Gessoriacum* (i.e. modern Boulogne), the closest crossing point on the continent. From there the focus, via Orosius, turns back to the north, the *Oceanus infinitus* and the Orkney Islands.[40]

Several earlier commentators have noted the mosaic nature of this opening chapter, in which Bede borrowed heavily from earlier geographical descriptions of Britain, and although one could easily sympathize with Charles Plummer's wish that 'Bede had given us more of his own observation and less of ancient writers', the choices he made in this chapter remain significant for being the result of careful selection.[41] Britain is first and foremost an island in the ocean, at a considerable distance from the European continent. Indications on where to cross the sea that separated the two, however, are promptly provided by combining the information given in Orosius (supplemented by the vernacular rendition of the Latin name for Richborough) with that found in Pliny.[42] Bede's careful weaving of different sources indicates that he perceived the island as separated from the main lands in Europe, especially given his reliance on Orosius to describe Britain primarily as an island in the ocean. At the same

---

[39] Merrills, *History and Geography*, 235–60.

[40] Colgrave and Mynors, eds. and trans., *Bede's Ecclesiastical History*, I.1, pp. 14–15 ('Quae per milia passuum DCCC in boream longa, latitudinis habet milia CC, exceptis dumtaxat prolixioribus diuersorum promontoriorum tractibus, quibus efficitur ut circuitus eius quadragies octies LXXV milia conpleat. Habet a meridie Galliam Belgicam, cuius proximum litus transmeantibus aperit ciuitas quae dicitur Rutubi portus, a gente Anglorum nunc corrupte Reptacaestir uocata, interposito mari a Gessoriaco Morynorum gentis litore proximo, traiectu milium L siue, ut quidam scripsere, stadiorum CCCCL. A tergo autem, unde Oceano infinito patet, Orcadas insulas habet'). A detailed reconstruction of Bede's borrowings is provided by *Fontes Anglo-Saxonici*, now available at https://arts.st-andrews.ac.uk/fontes/search. I am grateful to Dr Christine Rauer for providing access to the data ahead of the launch of the new website.

[41] Merrills, *History and Geography*, 249 n. 80.

[42] That Bede should have kept Orosius' reference to Richborough is also revealing of how much he relied on past sources rather than contemporary experience, given that in the early eighth century Richborough was not among the main ports normally used to connect Britain to the continent; see Section 7 below.

time, however, the European continent provides the key reference point for locating Britain, and the mention of the shortest crossing route between the two mitigates the sense of separation created by the chapter's opening lines.

Orosius' work continued to be influential in Anglo-Saxon England, and at some point between the late ninth and early tenth centuries an anonymous West Saxon scholar produced an Old English translation and adaptation of the *Historiae adversus paganos*.[43] A comparison between Bede's reliance on Orosius' account of the geography of the world and the later vernacular adaptation shows an interesting shift in perspective: in the Old English *Orosius* the emphasis on the ocean has disappeared and Britain is described as just another one of the territories forming part of Europe, following immediately after Spain.[44] Moreover, in the introductory section on the boundaries of the three main parts of the world (i.e. Asia, Europe and Africa), the western boundary of Europe is said to be Ireland, in a sentence which does not have any corresponding passage in the original Latin text.[45] As a result, Britain is pushed more firmly within the territories that make up Europe. Interestingly, this shift accords with what Helen Appleton has recently observed about the features of the Anglo-Saxon *mappa mundi* preserved in the eleventh-century Cotton Tiberius B.v, which is probably a copy of a larger tenth-century Anglo-Saxon map (see Figure 1).[46] According to Appleton, the map's features suggest that by the end of King Alfred's reign, Britain was no longer as remote as it had appeared to be in earlier geographical descriptions, including that contained in Bede's *Historia ecclesiastica*. Both the map and the Old English adaptation of Orosius' work incorporate new material on Scandinavia and reflect more recent West Saxon interests, as is made evident by the prominence given in the map to centres of power, trade and wealth in north-western Europe.[47] The Carolingian decline of the late ninth and early tenth centuries had created new opportunities, and the rise of Scandinavia as a centre of power resulted in north-

---

[43] Multiple authorship has also been suggested for this work; on this aspect and possible connections with the programme of translations promoted by King Alfred the Great, see Bately, 'The Old English *Orosius*'.

[44] Godden, ed. and trans., *The Old English History of the World*, I.1, pp. 50–1.

[45] Godden, ed. and trans., *The Old English History of the World*, I.1, pp. 26–7. See also Discenza, *Inhabited Spaces*, 64–5.

[46] Appleton, 'The Northern World'.

[47] Amid the new information included in the geographical section at the start of the Old English *Orosius*, there are the detailed accounts of the travels of two seafarers, Ohthere and Wulfstan (Godden, ed. and trans., *The Old English History of the World*, I.1, pp. 36–49); Appleton suggests that the former of the two, or something very much like it, was the source for the depiction of Scandinavia on the Cotton map (Appleton, 'The Northern World'). On Ohthere's account and the circumstances leading to its inclusion in the Old English *Orosius*, see also Allport, 'Home Thoughts of Abroad'.

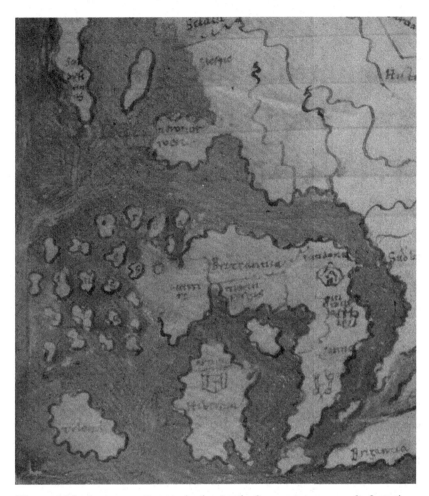

Figure 1 North-western Europe in the Anglo-Saxon *mappa mundi*, featuring relatively accurate outlines for Britain (*Brittannia*) and Ireland (*Hibernia*). Detail. London, British Library, Cotton Tiberius B.v, fol. 56v © The British Library Board

western Europe acquiring more importance both on the map and in the Old English *Orosius*.[48]

Anglo-Saxons' perceptions of their place in the world would thus seem to have shifted with time. While Bede's work reproduced late antique continental perspectives that placed Britain in a marginal north-western position, by the

---

[48] For a reading of the Old English *Orosius* as related to the theme of *translatio imperii*, that is, linking the demise of the Carolingians with the rise of Wessex, see Leneghan, '*Translatio imperii*'.

time of the Old English *Orosius* and the Cotton map, the north had acquired a new significance and could be represented and referred to with more confidence. This is not to say that early English writers had lost interest in places like Rome, which had always been central to 'the Anglo-Saxon mapping of Christian history', as Nicholas Howe put it in a very influential publication in which he described Rome as the 'capital of Anglo-Saxon England'.[49] It is in fact from there that one must begin, as no other place on the continent was as important to the Anglo-Saxons as Rome.

4 Rome and the Papacy

When dealing with the importance of Rome in early medieval England, one has the impression that, once again, it all started with Bede and the role he assigned in his *Historia ecclesiastica* to the mission sent by Pope Gregory the Great in 596 and led by the Roman monk Augustine, who became the first bishop of Canterbury. In Bede's narration, the pre-existing British church is described in negative terms, mostly because of its alleged refusal to convert the newly arrived pagan Anglo-Saxons,[50] while the efforts of the Irish missionaries who were active in Northumbria in the seventh century are duly acknowledged, even though they receive some indirect criticism for their position on the dating of Easter.[51] The synod of Whitby of 664, at which the Easter controversy was solved, is described as a triumph for the supporters of the Roman system of calculation – the one which Bede obviously considered correct – and the event which sealed the unity of the early English church.[52] Bede's championing of the Roman mission and his description of the subsequent relations between the English church and the papacy were informed by the accounts he obtained from his correspondents at Canterbury; indeed, the church of Canterbury can safely be described as the institution in England which most assiduously cultivated a continuous relationship with Rome throughout the Anglo-Saxon period. In the seventh century this extended to deliberate imitation of Rome through the reuse of Roman materials for the construction of the early churches in Canterbury, which were dedicated to saints with strong Roman links (e.g. Peter and Paul), and to the adoption of Roman liturgy.[53] Moreover, for almost a century after Augustine's arrival, all bishops of Canterbury were chosen by the popes and

---

[49] Howe, *Writing the Map of Anglo-Saxon England*, 104.

[50] On the limits of Bede's treatment of the British church, see Stancliffe, 'The British Church'.

[51] See most recently Yorke, 'Bede's Preferential Treatment of the Irish'.

[52] Wormald, 'The Venerable Bede'. For more recent studies and new interpretations of the synod's significance see Stancliffe, *Bede, Wilfrid, and the Irish*; Corning, *The Celtic and Roman Traditions*, 112–29; Dailey, 'To Choose One Easter'.

[53] Brooks, 'Canterbury and Rome'.

sent from Rome, with one very short-lived exception, Wighard, the first native English bishop-elect, who was sent to Rome in 667 or 668 to be consecrated by Pope Vitalian but died there of the plague.[54] At that point another man had to be found; famously, the pope's choice was Theodore, a monk originally from Tarsus in Cilicia, who was by then living in Rome. Theodore's pontificate at Canterbury (669–90) brought about changes in the organization, liturgy and learning of the early English church whose effects would be long-lasting. Among other things, Theodore was responsible for the introduction of a new model of metropolitan authority for the see at Canterbury through his adoption of the title of archbishop and the grant of the archiepiscopal pallium from the pope, which was accompanied by the right to consecrate bishops in his province.[55] The pallium was a white woollen band marked with crosses which could be worn for the celebration of the Mass on specific days and came to represent an archbishop's principal symbol of authority derived from the papacy (see Figure 2).

In 735 Bishop Ecgbert of York also received the pallium from the then Pope Gregory II. With the institution of the archbishopric of York, the ecclesiastical map of Anglo-Saxon England now comprised two provinces, but the Canterbury archiepiscopal incumbents appear to have been always more active than their northern colleagues in cultivating the special bond that linked them to Rome through the pallium.[56] Indeed, from the early decades of the tenth until the mid-eleventh century, all archbishops-elect of Canterbury went to Rome in person to fetch this liturgical garb from the pope, at a time when the papacy did not yet require such a practice. The best known of these trips is that of Archbishop Sigeric, who went to fetch his pallium in 990 and kept a diary of the churches he visited while in the Eternal City and of the itinerary of his return journey.[57] The late Anglo-Saxon archbishops of York followed their Canterbury colleagues in this practice but do not seem to have been as assiduous.

In the late Anglo-Saxon period, the archbishop of Canterbury was also the final link in the network which was put in place to collect an annual payment to the papacy later known as Peter's Pence. Normally called *Rompenincg* ('Rome penny') or *Romfeoh* ('Rome money') in Old English sources, this payment

---

[54] Brooks, *The Early History of the Church of Canterbury*, 69–70.

[55] Thacker, 'Gallic or Greek?' On Theodore see also Lapidge, ed., *Archbishop Theodore*. In the eighth century this model was then exported to the continent thanks to the English missionaries Willibrord and Boniface: Schoenig, *Bonds of Wool*, 11–13; Schieffer, 'Boniface', 16–17. On the English missions to the continent, see Section 6 below.

[56] Tinti, 'The Archiepiscopal Pallium'.

[57] Ortenberg, 'Archbishop Sigeric's Journey to Rome'; Tinti, 'The English Presence'. See also Section 7 below.

Figure 2 Archbishop Dunstan of Canterbury wearing his pallium. Detail. London, British Library, Cotton Tiberius A.iii, fol. 2v © The British Library Board

consisted of one penny from every household in England.[58] In this case too, one witnesses the Anglo-Saxon origins of a phenomenon which would later extend to other regions in Europe and in which the Canterbury see played a major role. This is not to say, however, that Canterbury was the only institution in England to pursue a close relationship with Rome. In fact, on various occasions it is possible to observe other powerful agents seeking papal support to counteract Canterbury's interests. One of the most famous and controversial cases was that concerning Bishop Wilfrid, who appealed directly to the pope after he was driven from his Northumbrian see in 678. He sought papal help again when in 703 a synod presided over by Archbishop Berhtwald of Canterbury suspended him from episcopal office. On both occasions the papacy tried to find a middle

---

[58] Naismith and Tinti, 'The Origins of Peter's Pence'.

way, probably in order to avoid a major crisis in its relations with either of the parties involved.[59]

Occasionally one has the impression that the popes found it difficult to navigate such situations. A major incident occurred between the end of the eighth century and the start of the ninth, when a third archbishopric was established at Lichfield. It had the approval of Pope Hadrian I, but was seemingly the brainchild of the powerful King Offa of Mercia, who was eager to overcome the opposition of Archbishop Jænberht of Canterbury to the anointing of Offa's son Ecgfrith and, more generally, to ensure episcopal cooperation in the king's attempt to achieve a Carolingian-style polity.[60] The most interesting and revealing account of these events is provided by the letter that Pope Leo III sent in 798 to Offa's successor, Coenwulf. In this letter, the pope stated that Pope Hadrian, his predecessor, had agreed to the division of the Canterbury province because Offa had 'testified in his letter that it was the united wish and unanimous position of all of you, both on account of the vast size of your lands and the extension of your kingdom, and for many more reasons and benefits'.[61] The letter's tone hints at the pope's frustration with a complex and evolving political situation in a far-off land, one in which papal authority was repeatedly called upon to solve conflicts. The incident shows that the see of Canterbury, notwithstanding its actively cultivated links with Rome, also had to come to terms with other, often more powerful players perfectly capable of making the papacy act in their favour.

So far, we have mainly discussed instances in which the Anglo-Saxons sought the popes' interventions, or, as in the cases of Peter's Pence and the personal fetching of the archiepiscopal pallium, customs that anticipated practices which later extended to other territories in the Christian West. But what can one say about the papacy's interest in the Anglo-Saxons? In what circumstances can one see the popes promoting relations with them? If we go back to what Bede identifies as the origins of English Christianity, that is the mission sent by Gregory the Great in 596, we can certainly observe active papal engagement, irrespective of whether the famous story about Gregory seeing English slave boys in a Roman market was really what triggered his missionary initiative.[62] The pope's correspondence shows that he followed the mission's progress closely and had reasons to rejoice about the missionaries' achievements among the *Angli*.[63] His immediate successors' letters to recipients in England

---

[59] Ó Carragáin and Thacker, 'Wilfrid in Rome'.

[60] Noble, 'The Rise and Fall of the Archbishopric of Lichfield'.

[61] Whitelock, ed., *English Historical Documents*, no. 205.

[62] Markus, *Gregory the Great*, 177–8.

[63] Markus, *Gregory the Great*, 179, 186 n. 100. Gregory regularly used the ethnonym *Angli* in his correspondence, a choice that has been ascribed to his adoption of Byzantine terminology,

display similar interest, both in the progress of the mission and the organization of the nascent English church.[64] It is probably safe to say that for no other period of Anglo-Saxon history do the available sources allow one to identify a level of papal interest in the English church comparable to what can be observed in these early years. Other significant occasions can be identified later on, as was the case in 786 when, for the first time since the Gregorian mission, papal legates were sent to England. However, the report drafted by one of the legates – Bishop George of Ostia – is not particularly informative about the original purpose of the legatine mission. Catherine Cubitt has observed that in traditional analyses of the mission and the various councils in which the legates participated, scholars have generally focused on the situation in Mercia and the possibility that Offa may have used the presence of the legates in England to facilitate the creation of the archbishopric of Lichfield. But the visit also involved a council that met in Northumbria, and by shifting one's attention towards this northern gathering and the contents of the canons that it issued, one can appreciate that the internal affairs of this kingdom, with its record of aristocratic factions, conspiracies, kings' depositions and murder, may have contributed to the papal decision to send legates to England.[65] There were probably multiple reasons for their despatch, but since papal correspondence makes no mention of the legation itself, it is not possible to identify what exactly prompted the pope to send it and how its outcomes were received in Rome.[66]

Papal interest in the Anglo-Saxons, at least until the end of the ninth century, can be appreciated closer to home through the evidence provided by a compilation of biographies of popes known as *Liber pontificalis*.[67] From the second half of the eighth century the biographies incorporate references to the *scholae peregrinorum* of various ethnic groups, namely the Franks, the Frisians, the Lombards and the *Saxones*, that is, the Anglo-Saxons.[68] The *scholae peregrinorum* were foundations located near the Vatican which hosted

---

probably because of the years he spent as *apocrisiarius* in Constantinople: Pohl, 'Ethnic Names and Identities', 19.

[64] See Hunter Blair, 'The Letters of Pope Boniface V', and Story, 'Bede, Willibrord and the Letters of Pope Honorius I'.

[65] Cubitt, *Anglo-Saxon Church Councils*, 153–90.

[66] Uncertainties also emerge when analysing the reasons for sending another papal legate to England two centuries later, in 990. The aim in this case was the conclusion of a peace treaty between the king of England and the duke of Normandy; however, while traditional interpretations have read the treaty as a response to the danger posed by Norman harbouring of viking raiders, Jenny Benham has recently demonstrated that this cannot have been the reason for the hostility between the two rulers: Benham, 'The Earliest Arbitration Treaty?'

[67] For a recent study see McKitterick, *Rome and the Invention of the Papacy*.

[68] On the origins of the *scholae peregrinorum* see most recently Santangeli Valenzani, 'Hosting Foreigners'; on the persistence of the 'Saxon' element to refer to the English quarter in Rome, see Tinti, 'The English Presence'.

foreigners living in Rome and provided assistance and accommodation to pilgrims belonging to the same ethnic group. Their exact dates of foundation cannot be identified, and it is likely that foreigners from the same country started to gather in specific districts before the formal institution of the *scholae peregrinorum*. The *Liber pontificalis* indicates that in the eighth and ninth centuries the *scholae* included military units which were deployed on various occasions, including when, in 846, they were sent to Portus, the harbour of Rome located on the mouth of the Tiber river, to defend the city from Saracen attacks.[69] While in this specific instance the reference is to the 'Saxi et Frisones et schola quae dicitur Francorum', on a number of other occasions the attention of the popes' biographers focuses specifically on the English in Rome, especially the buildings in their quarter, located by the right bank of the Tiber on the site currently occupied by the Complesso monumentale di Santo Spirito in Sassia (see Figure 3).

An example is provided by the biography of Pope Paschal I, in a chapter describing the terrible consequences of a fire which in 817 destroyed the English quarter (or *burgus*, as it was already called).[70] The pope is said to have hastened there on horseback without even putting his shoes on, and his presence on the site miraculously stopped the fire from expanding further. Afterwards, he made numerous donations (of gold, silver, clothes, food and timber) to help the *peregrini* recover from the losses inflicted by the fire. The papacy's continued interest in the *burgus* is confirmed later on by the actions of another pope, Leo IV, who in 847 miraculously extinguished yet another fire in the *Saxorum vicus*.[71] In a subsequent passage of the same biography Leo is also said to have built (or perhaps rebuilt) from the ground the church of St Mary 'over the *schola Saxonum*'.[72]

Papal financial support of this scale must be placed within the more general framework of the popes' patronage of numerous construction and restoration projects in and around Rome at this time. As several studies have shown, between the second half of the eighth century and the first half of the ninth there seems to have been more wealth in Rome than before or after, and much of this wealth was most likely related to the high number of visitors (pilgrims and ecclesiastics) who made their way to the Eternal City, especially from northern

---

[69] Duchesne, ed., *Liber Pontificalis*, II, p. 100; Davis, trans., *The Lives of the Ninth-Century Popes*, 95.

[70] Duchesne, ed., *Liber Pontificalis*, II, pp. 53–4; Davis, trans., *The Lives of the Ninth-Century Popes*, 8–9. This event is also recorded in the Anglo-Saxon Chronicle.

[71] Duchesne, ed., *Liber Pontificalis*, II, pp. 110–11; Davis, trans., *The Lives of the Ninth-Century Popes*, 119.

[72] Duchesne, ed., *Liber Pontificalis*, I, p. 128; Davis, trans., *The Lives of the Ninth-Century Popes*, 148.

Figure 3 Complesso monumentale di S. Spirito in Sassia, Rome. Photo: Francesca Tinti

Europe. These brought with them plenty of donations, but they also participated in the lively market of luxury goods available there.[73] The popes' interest in and support for the *schola Saxonum* may well have taken account of the significant role the Anglo-Saxons played in the circulation of money and precious objects that took place in Rome: in the period between *c.*780 and *c.*850, English coins represent a major proportion of numismatic finds in Rome and Italy.[74] Furthermore, among the valuable objects which, according to the *Liber pontificalis*, eighth- and ninth-century popes are known to have donated to numerous churches in Rome, there are a total of 277 precious bowls called *gabatae*, probably used as lamp fittings and ornaments; of these, a subset of 19 items are described as *gabatae saxiscae*. Whenever their material is also specified, they are said to be silver bowls, whose patterned decoration probably distinguished them as 'Saxon' (i.e. English).[75] These were most likely gifts from English donors, which the popes redistributed to various churches in Rome.

---

[73] Delogu, 'The Rebirth of Rome'; Goodson, *The Rome of Paschal I*, 67–8.

[74] Naismith, 'Peter's Pence and Before'.

[75] Gem, '*Gabatae saxiscae*'. A further group of twelve bowls of *opus anglorum*, attested in the pontificate of Gregory IV (827–44) can probably be added to the total. Cf. Gem, '*Gabatae saxiscae*', 93 and Davis, trans., *The Lives of the Ninth-Century Popes*, 54 n. 20.

The most remarkable example of donations from an English pilgrim recorded in the *Liber pontificalis* appears within the biography of Benedict III (855–8), with reference to the West Saxon King Æthelwulf, who was in Rome in 855. The list of gifts made by the king to St Peter includes several precious metal objects, such as a golden crown, a sword bound with fine gold, two golden beakers and four 'gabathe saxisce de argento exaurate' ('silver-gilt Saxon bowls'), as well as various fine silk liturgical vestments and drapes of Byzantine origin, which the king had probably bought in Rome. Æthelwulf is also said to have distributed gold and silver to the clergy and leading men of the city and further silver to the people of Rome. His display of piety and generosity can be compared with the various donations made by Charlemagne in Rome, especially that following his imperial coronation in 800, which also included several silver and golden objects. Charlemagne's well-recorded munificence may have acted as a source of inspiration for Æthelwulf.[76]

Piety and the display of power clearly went hand in hand in such public demonstrations of generosity and are indicative of the wider significance and political implications of the journeys to Rome of early medieval rulers, magnates and higher ecclesiastics. In some exceptional circumstances, these could result in truly grand occasions, as was the case for King Cnut, who was in Rome in 1027 to attend the coronation of Emperor Conrad II. Several scholars have observed that the imperial connotations of the image which Cnut began to cultivate shortly afterwards may have been inspired by what he had witnessed in Rome. The tone of the letter that he wrote to his English subjects after attending the ceremony would seem to indicate that he was rather impressed by the event and the meetings he had attended there with the emperor, the pope, Rudolf, king of Burgundy and the other European rulers who were present.[77]

Diplomatic missions to Rome could also result, however, in fairly dramatic turns of events, perhaps most memorably for the party of secular magnates and senior ecclesiastics who made their way to the Eternal City in 1061. They were led by Earl Tostig, who was also accompanied by his wife, Judith of Flanders and by a number of bishops, including Ealdred, bishop of Worcester and archbishop-elect of York, who went to Rome to receive his archiepiscopal pallium from Pope Nicholas II. Not only did the pope deny Ealdred the pallium, because of his having irregularly moved from one episcopal see to another; but also, subsequently the party was attacked and robbed not long after setting out from Rome on their way back home. This obliged them to

---

[76] Schieffer, 'Charlemagne and Rome', 289–95; Thomas, 'Three Welsh Kings', 565.

[77] Bolton, *The Empire of Cnut*, 294–303; Treharne, *Living through Conquest*, 28–43. See also Section 8 below.

change their plans and go back to the city, where the pope, moved to compassion, decided to grant Ealdred the pallium on condition that he renounced the Worcester see.[78]

Although Ealdred and his companions' vicissitudes were undoubtedly exceptional, visiting Rome must have been a memorable and demanding experience for all early medieval English visitors. The support provided by the *schola Saxonum* will have been crucial in terms of assistance and guidance, but in spite of the presence of this institution, as well as the eagerness with which the journey from England to the thresholds of the apostles was generally undertaken,[79] difficulties of various kinds can be identified in several accounts on the Anglo-Saxons in Rome. Among these, it is not surprising to encounter language issues. Willibald, St Boniface's biographer, reports that when Boniface went to Rome to meet Pope Gregory II in 722, he was questioned on his Christian credentials, and he asked in response if he could produce a written profession of faith because he did not feel comfortable speaking the pope's language. As Roger Wright has observed, the main issue at stake does not seem to have been mutual intelligibility, as the two had already met on a previous occasion and seem to have been able to talk to each other without major difficulties.[80] Boniface's reluctance to make his profession of faith orally seems to be instead related to the delicacy of the matter, which he felt he could address more securely in writing. The pope's spoken language, which Boniface felt he could not master, was that of a native Romance speaker, which would have sounded different from the Latin that the Englishman had learnt as a foreign language.

Rome could present even more linguistically challenging situations for the Anglo-Saxon traveller because of its cosmopolitan nature and multilingual environment. Less than twenty years earlier, in 704, the above-mentioned Wilfrid was in Rome to appeal against Archbishop Berhtwald's decision to suspend him from the exercise of his episcopal office. The matter was addressed at a synod presided over by Pope John VI. In his description of the meeting, Stephen of Ripon – Wilfrid's biographer – says that having heard the evidence provided by representatives of the archbishop, as well as Wilfrid's defence, 'they [i.e. those participating in the synod] began to talk Greek among themselves and to smile covertly, saying many things which they concealed from us'.[81] Stephen's frustration and sense of exclusion is palpable: John VI was

---

[78] Tinti, 'The Pallium Privilege of Pope Nicholas II'.

[79] As repeatedly attested by Bede: Wallis, trans., *Bede: The Reckoning of Time*, 236; Colgrave and Mynors, eds. and trans., *Bede's Ecclesiastical History*, V.7, pp. 472–3.

[80] Wright, *A Sociophilological Study of Late Latin*, 95–109.

[81] Colgrave, ed. and trans., *The Life of Bishop Wilfrid*, c. 53, p. 113.

Greek and many of the prelates attending the synod would have also been Greek speakers, as Greek elites had a significant presence in Rome at this time: Wilfrid and Stephen, as well as the representatives of Archbishop Berhtwald, were probably not expecting the exclusionary code-switching that they experienced in the course of the meeting.[82] But just as the English could easily be made to feel foreign in Rome through the use of a language that they did not know, we have some indirect evidence of the kind of uncertain and confused reaction that their native language could also cause. This is provided by a later source, namely the eleventh-century Life of St Kenelm probably written by Goscelin of St-Bertin, in a passage referring to the miraculous delivery on the altar of St Peter's in Rome of a letter inscribed with golden characters in a language which the pope, who was celebrating mass at that very moment, could not understand. After enquiring among the peoples of the many nations who were flocking to St Peter's, he found help among those who were staying at the *Anglica scola* (i.e. the *schola Saxonum*, which by Goscelin's time was being referred to, at least in England, through different ethnic labelling).[83] Although the event referred to in the Life is supposed to have taken place in the ninth century, the language employed is more likely to reflect eleventh-century conditions, which suggests that the people residing in the English quarter at that time may have acted as interpreters when such a need arose.

The Anglo-Saxons residing in Rome could also attract the attention of the locals for other reasons. A fragmentary text of a letter sent in the 870s by Pope John VIII to the archbishops of Canterbury and York and all the clergy in England says that the Englishmen living in Rome near St Peter's (presumably meaning at the *schola Saxonum*) had assembled to discuss the lay habit worn by the English clerics, and decided that the latter would abandon their short garments and clothe themselves in clerical tunics that reached to the ankle, according to the Roman fashion.[84] While criticism of ostentatious clerical dress is fairly frequent in the sources from our period, this specific reference to Anglo-Saxon ecclesiastics in Rome standing out because of their clothes, which made them look like secular men, is suggestive of the ways in which a group of foreigners could be perceived as 'different'. Interestingly, the Anglo-Saxons in general, rather than churchmen specifically, had already attracted the attention of the Lombard writer Paul the Deacon in the late eighth century because of their loose linen clothes, embellished with borders

---

[82] On Stephen's accompanying Wilfrid to Rome on his last journey there, see Colgrave, ed. and trans., *The Life of Bishop Wilfrid*, x.

[83] Love, ed. and trans., *Three Eleventh-Century Anglo-Latin Saints' Lives*, 64–7. For further discussion see Tinti, 'The English Presence'.

[84] Whitelock, ed., *English Historical Documents*, no. 221.

woven in various colours.[85] Dress is, of course, one of the principal markers
of identity in a person's appearance, one which can make people immediately
look foreign or simply out of place. Judging by the remarks of both Paul the
Deacon and John VIII, Anglo-Saxon clothes clearly attracted attention.
Maureen Miller has also recently suggested that the Anglo-Saxons played
an important role in the promotion of highly ornate liturgical garb (as
opposed to 'streetwear') adorned with gold, which seems to have become
acceptable and even desired by Carolingian liturgists in the course of the
ninth century.[86] The new style reached Italy relatively late, but if Miller is
right in seeing its origins in the Anglo-Saxons' taste for ornament, we would
be witnessing a significant manifestation of cultural transmission between
England and the continent in which the former would have played a much
more active role than is normally acknowledged.

5 Courts, Diplomacy and Dynasties

Clerical dress also figures in a letter that Alcuin wrote in 801 to Archbishop
Æthelheard of Canterbury ahead of the latter's visit to Charlemagne's court on
his way to Rome. Alcuin was very specific about Æthelheard having to warn
those accompanying him, especially the clerics, on the need to attend to religious observance in their choice of clothes. He was particularly eager to let them
know that they should not wear gold or silk vestments in the king's presence.[87]
Here we can see Alcuin acting as a cultural mediator, knowing both the habits
and tastes of his fellow countrymen and the prevailing attitudes at the
Carolingian court, where clerics wearing ostentatious garments were frowned
upon, just as seems to have been the case in Rome later on during John VIII's
pontificate.

In spite of the potential for friction due to different practices, insular scholars
were numerous and welcome at the court of Charlemagne.[88] Although the
evidence for Alcuin's fame and closeness to the king eclipses that for other
English and Irishmen who were active there from the 780s onwards, it is
important not to underestimate the influence of the insular presence as
a whole at the Carolingian court. Charlemagne trusted several of those men
with diplomatic missions, as was the case for Candidus, an English student of
Alcuin's who was sent to Rome at least twice at the turn of the ninth century to

---

[85] See Section 2 above. See also Owen-Crocker, *Dress in Anglo-Saxon England*, 171–8 and Miller,
Clothing the Clergy, 132.

[86] Miller, *Clothing the Clergy*, 126–33.   [87] Miller, *Clothing the Clergy*, 115.

[88] It has been observed that Charlemagne's willingness to patronize many scholars from distant
lands should be interpreted as the result of a sincere belief in the duty of hospitality: Garrison,
'The English and the Irish'.

investigate a crisis surrounding Pope Leo III.[89] In this area too, however, most of the information at our disposal concerns Alcuin, who was sent to England on at least two occasions on behalf of the Frankish king. Alcuin's first journey back to his native country was prompted by the above-mentioned legatine mission of 786, which Alcuin joined in Northumbria before accompanying the party back to Mercia.[90] His second journey took place in the early 790s, when he acted as mediator in a number of delicate matters between Charlemagne and King Offa of Mercia, including the breakdown of negotiations for a marriage alliance between a son of the Carolingian ruler and Offa's daughter.[91] It would seem that the same daughter of Offa then got married to Æthelred of Northumbria in September 792, an event which according to some scholars may be interpreted as the result of Alcuin's mediation.[92] The negotiations had halted abruptly when Offa suggested a parallel marriage between his son Ecgfrith and one of Charlemagne's daughters. This has been seen by several historians as a sign of Offa's excessive ambition. Offa would obviously have gained in prestige and power by having the direct offspring of the most powerful dynasty in Europe at his court in Mercia, but he probably miscalculated the extent to which Charlemagne was prepared to be seen as on a par with the Mercian king.[93]

Marriage alliances were often at the centre of diplomatic relations between early medieval dynasties.[94] In fact, even the earliest forms of connection between Anglo-Saxon and continental royal courts, dating back to the late sixth and seventh centuries, were initially forged through marriage, as was the case with the Frankish princess Bertha who married Æthelberht of Kent in the second half of the sixth century, probably before he became king. The movement of royal women went in both directions, as there is evidence for seventh-century Frankish queens of Anglo-Saxon origin.[95] Half a century after the diplomatic crisis between Charlemagne and Offa, King Æthelwulf of Wessex married Judith, daughter of Charles the Bald and great-granddaughter of Charlemagne, on his way back from Rome in 856. Scholars have striven to explain the reasons for this union and a number of hypotheses have been advanced, including the possibility that the marriage was meant to cement an alliance between the Franks and the Anglo-Saxons to

---

[89] Garrison, 'The English and the Irish'; Story, *Carolingian Connections*, 257. On Candidus' life and career see most recently Jones, 'An Edition of the Four Sermons', 7–12. Interestingly Pope Leo III also employed a legate of Anglo-Saxon origin ('de Brittania, natione Saxo') called Aldulf in the early ninth century: Nelson, 'England and the Continent in the Ninth Century', 18–20.

[90] Story, *Carolingian Connections*, 61–4.

[91] For reservations on the reliability of the account of this marriage alliance preserved in the *Gesta abbatum Fontanellensium*, see McKitterick, *Charlemagne*, 282–4.

[92] Story, *Carolingian Connections*, 136.   [93] Nelson, *King and Emperor*, 270–1.

[94] For a general study see Stafford, *Queens, Concubines and Dowagers*.

[95] Wood, 'The Continental Connections'.

fight the vikings.[96] Whatever the reason (or reasons) behind the marriage, it is clear that the reservations Charlemagne felt about letting his daughters marry a foreign prince or ruler (and an English one more specifically) were not shared by Charles the Bald on this occasion.[97]

Later on, such marriage alliances intensified, especially during the reigns of Edward the Elder and Æthelstan, when as many as four of the former's daughters married into continental families.[98] Particularly remarkable was the marriage in 929 or 930 between Æthelstan's half-sister, Eadgyth (or Edith), and Otto, son of the East Frankish king Henry I. By this time the house of Wessex enjoyed international fame thanks to its military success against the vikings, while the Carolingian Empire had disintegrated through internal crises and Scandinavian attacks.[99] Of course, Carolingian ideas of kingship had contributed to the rise of the house of Wessex, starting in 853 with the papal anointing of Alfred in Rome as a child, as reported by the Anglo-Saxon Chronicle and Asser's Life of Alfred. The reliability of these accounts, as well as the actual nature of the anointing ceremony, have been the object of lively scholarly debates, but if the anointing did take place, it was likely inspired by earlier Carolingian ceremonies meant to consecrate future rulers.[100]

Eadgyth's marriage to Otto was discussed by several tenth-century commentators, both English and continental, who registered its significance by stressing her royal lineage.[101] Both Æthelweard's Chronicle and Hrotsvitha's *Gesta Ottonis* refer to the fact that Æthelstan actually sent two of his sisters (Eadgyth and Ælfgifu) to Otto in Saxony, so that he could choose his bride.[102] Interestingly, however, it would seem that the initiative to find a suitable match for Otto abroad came from his father, Henry I, who had previously sent envoys to Æthelstan to start negotiations for a marriage alliance. Once again we can see how power dynamics had changed, aspirations had evolved and perceptions had shifted: the West Saxon dynasty had longer- and better-established royal credentials than Henry I's family. At this stage of the latter's ascendancy, marriage

---

[96] The term 'viking' is spelt with lowercase 'v' following recent developments in historiography which have emphasized that the Old English term from which it derives (*wicing*) was used to translate Latin *pirata* and did not have an ethnic connotation; see Cross, *Heirs of the Vikings*, xii.

[97] Story, *Carolingian Connections*, 240–3. For the argument that the initiative behind the marriage alliance came from Charles see Nelson, *Charles the Bald*, 182; but cf. Stafford, 'Charles the Bald', 140.

[98] Foot, *Æthelstan*, 44–52.

[99] Ortenberg, '"The King from Overseas"'; Wood, 'A Carolingian Scholar', 136.

[100] Story, *Carolingian Connections*, 236–7.

[101] On the 'deeply felt sense of connectedness between English and Continental affairs' emanating from these and later sources dealing with Otto and Eadgyth's marriage, see MacLean, *Ottonian Queenship*, 29.

[102] Foot, *Æthelstan*, 48–52.

into the West Saxon royal family was deemed beneficial in securing Otto's succession to the kingship and strengthening the Ottonians' political stance vis-à-vis their competitors in West Francia.[103]

Eadgyth and Ælfgifu were accompanied to East Francia by Bishop Cenwald of Worcester with lavish gifts for the king and the monasteries that the bishop visited in the course of his trip.[104] Cenwald's diplomatic mission of 929 cemented relationships between England and the continent, also thanks to the spiritual connections which were then established, as attested by a short text entered in a manuscript preserved at the abbey of St Gall in modern Switzerland (St Gallen, Stiftsbibliothek, Cod. Sang. 915).[105] It says that Bishop Cenwald had visited 'all the monasteries throughout Germany', making substantial offerings of silver that had been entrusted to him by the king of the English. He stayed at the monastery of St Gall for four days in October 929 and celebrated with the monks the feast of their patron saint. The community promised to remember him in their prayers as they did with their own members, both living and dead. The text closes by listing eight people whose names Cenwald wanted the monks to record so that they could offer prayers for all of them; these included King Æthelstan, Cenwald himself and possibly, judging by the form of their names, a number of the latter's relatives. The same people were included in a longer list of English names which, on the same occasion, were entered in a confraternity book of St Gall (St Gallen, Stiftsarchiv, C3 B55). In this case the name of the king is followed by that of Wulfhelm, archbishop of Canterbury, several other contemporary English bishops, two abbots, twelve more people of uncertain identity (who may have formed part of Cenwald's party) and, finally, all the names which, together with that of Cenwald, had been recorded in the other St Gall manuscript describing the bishop's visit to 'Germany'.[106] An interesting aspect of this relatively long list of names is the spelling employed, which follows contemporary continental Germanic usage rather than Old English conventions, thus indicating that the names recorded were communicated orally by Cenwald to a scribe at St Gall, who would have then proceeded to write them down in accordance with the orthographic custom he was more familiar with (e.g. *Conrat* instead of *Coenred*).[107]

---

[103] Leyser, 'The Ottonians and Wessex'; Stafford, *Queens, Concubines and Dowagers*, 34–5; MacLean, *Ottonian Queenship*, 28–37.

[104] Foot, *Æthelstan*, 101–2; Keynes, 'King Athelstan's Books'.

[105] This is available online at www.e-codices.unifr.ch/en/csg/0915/5/0/Sequence-714.

[106] Keynes, 'King Athelstan's Books', 198–201.

[107] A contemporary entry in the confraternity book of Reichenau, not far from St Gall, can probably also be related to Cenwald's trip of 929, even though the bishop himself is not named in this case; Keynes, 'King Athelstan's Books', 200.

Confraternity books, also called *libri vitae*, were kept by several early medieval religious communities, both on the continent and in England. They contain long lists of people's names, normally ranging from members of the institution where the book originated to their benefactors and members of other religious communities to whom they were bound by confraternity agreements, that is via promises of reciprocal prayer. The presence of English names in continental *libri vitae* attests to the far-reaching religious, social and political dimensions of diplomatic trips to the continent such as that of Cenwald. Their importance should not be underestimated: to have one's name recorded in confraternity books meant ensuring one's entry into wide networks of perpetual prayer and commemorative rituals. Both at St Gall and at Reichenau, the two religious communities which recorded English names in their confraternity books in connection with Cenwald's trip of 929, such commemorative practices had their origin in the Carolingian period, when intercessory monastic prayer acquired a pivotal role in the creation of vast social and political alliances.[108]

Relationships between England and Germany remained close throughout Æthelstan's reign, as attested by the international encounters which took place at his court.[109] The king's entourage comprised several scholars and clerics of German provenance who would have mingled with Frankish messengers, Breton political and ecclesiastical exiles, Welsh kings, Irish clerics and Scandinavian visitors. Such a wide circulation of people at Æthelstan's cosmopolitan court was matched by an equally wide movement of books, relics, artefacts and ideas.[110] Tenth-century literary production in England was clearly influenced by those exchanges: the Latin poem mentioning Æthelstan and opening with the words 'Carta dirige gressus' may have been written by a scholar of continental origin named Petrus, who modelled it on an earlier Latin poem for Charlemagne.[111] A possible continental author has also been suggested for another Latin poem in praise of Æthelstan, which was copied at Christ Church Canterbury in a gospel book (also of continental origin) that the

---

[108] McKitterick, *History and Memory*, 162–72; Hendrix, 'The Confraternity Books of St Gall'. This was not the first time that Anglo-Saxon people made their appearance in continental confraternity books, as several English names were also entered in the ninth century in the *liber vitae* of Brescia: Keynes, 'Anglo-Saxon Entries'.

[109] Foot, *Æthelstan*, 91–3, 99–110; Wood, 'A Carolingian Scholar'.

[110] Wood, 'The Making of King Æthelstan's Empire'; Keynes, 'King Athelstan's Books'; Foot, *Æthelstan*, 91–126; Zacher, 'Multilingualism at the Court of King Æthelstan', with bibliography there cited.

[111] Lapidge, 'Some Latin Poems', 71–81. The hypothesis, also suggested by Lapidge in the same article, that an eight-line acrostic praise-poem in honour of Æthelstan was written by John the Old Saxon, a scholar who had come to England during Alfred's reign, has been more recently challenged in Gallagher, 'Latin Acrostic Poetry'.

king himself had given to the community there.[112] Furthermore, literary scholars have detected the influence of contemporary Norse poetry in the composition of the vernacular verses on Æthelstan's victory at the battle of Brunanburh of 937, which were included in the Anglo-Saxon Chronicle.[113]

The intersections of dynastic politics, multilingualism and international literary patronage became even more pronounced in the course of the eleventh century, as has recently been shown by Elizabeth Tyler, who has also highlighted the important role that English royal women played in the development of literary culture in Europe.[114] In particular, the movements through dynastic marriages of women such as Emma, daughter of Duke Richard of Normandy, or Edith, sister of Harold Godwineson, had a profound effect on eleventh-century historical writing. This was a time of dramatic change, as exemplified by Cnut's conquest of England in 1016; his marriage to the Norman Emma (who had previously been married to Æthelred the Unready); the restoration of the earlier English dynasty with the accession of Edward the Confessor (Emma's son by Æthelred), who had spent a long time in Normandy before acceding to the English throne in 1042; the latter's marriage to Edith; the very brief reign of her brother Harold; and the Norman Conquest of 1066. Amid the complex interweaving of dynastic politics generated by this succession of pivotal events, Latin historical writing at the Anglo-Saxon court was particularly vibrant, and royal women played a crucial role commissioning works such as the *Encomium Emmae reginae* and the *Vita Ædwardi regis*, through which both their clerical authors (of probable continental origin) and their female patrons negotiated competing accounts of conquest, political factions and internal struggles.

The multilingual and multicultural environment which characterized the English court in the eleventh century probably had its roots in the transformative educational programme initiated by King Alfred in the second half of the ninth century.[115] By the end of the Anglo-Saxon period, however, that environment had acquired a whole set of unprecedented features, thanks to the wider geographical range of connections brought about by military conquests and dynastic marriages. Within this new political and cultural landscape, royal women like Emma and Edith were at the centre of networks facilitating the creation of novel international alliances, the movement of aristocratic elites across political and linguistic borders and the promotion of a Latin literary

---

[112] Lapidge, 'Some Latin Poems', 81–5.   [113] Foot, *Æthelstan*, 112–14.

[114] Tyler, *England in Europe*; see also Stafford, *Queen Emma and Queen Edith*.

[115] The literature on this topic is vast. Useful insights on the international nature of Alfred's court culture can be found in several of the essays collected in Nelson, *Rulers and Ruling Families*. See also Scharer, 'The Writing of History at King Alfred's Court'.

culture which attracted secular audiences. On the eve of the Norman Conquest, the English court was already deeply embedded within Europe.[116]

6 Missions and Monasticism

If marriage alliances, diplomatic trips and ambitious literary patronage generated occasions for the mingling of Anglo-Saxon and continental elites and reconfigured political allegiances across Europe, parallel activities and initiatives in the religious sphere opened the way to many other, often longer-lasting relations between England and the continent. Indeed, the two areas – secular and religious – should not be thought of as separate, given their markedly intertwined relationship, demonstrated, for instance, by the significant spiritual connections which Bishop Cenwald established, on his own and on King Æthelstan's behalf, with several religious continental communities in the course of his diplomatic journey to Germany. Similarly, the Roman and Irish missions which, according to Bede's account, brought Christianity to England could prosper because of leading Anglo-Saxon secular elites' support and patronage.

In the case of the Roman mission, crucial resources in terms of support and hospitality were also provided to Augustine and his companions – while on their way to Britain – by the Merovingian ruling family, as attested by the letters that Gregory the Great wrote between 596 and 601 to various recipients in Gaul.[117] Several scholars have observed that the sources for the study of the Roman mission and the subsequent conversion of the Anglo-Saxons reveal a wider context in which it is possible to identify some form of Frankish overlordship in southern England.[118] Its nature and extent are not easy to pin down and it is possible that surviving sources reflect more closely Frankish aspirations than actual domination.[119] In any case, there is no denying Merovingian involvement in Anglo-Saxon affairs at this time, and the presence of Frankish objects in Kentish burials attests to significant cultural influence as well as sustained cross-Channel trade.[120] It has been suggested that this Frankish connection was especially important for the conversion of kings in southern England. When the Merovingian princess Bertha, daughter of the Frankish king Charibert I, got married to Æthelberht, son of the king of Kent, she was dispatched there with a bishop named Liudhard. Most commentators have assumed that he was the princess's chaplain, but the choice of a bishop may indicate that he did not just have private responsibilities and that Æthelberht was

---

[116] Tyler, 'Crossing Conquests'.   [117] Wood, 'Augustine and Gaul'.
[118] The hypothesis was first presented in Wood, *The Merovingian North Sea*.
[119] Brookes, *Economics and Social Change in Anglo-Saxon Kent*, p. 8. See also Halsall, *Worlds of Arthur*, 283–5.
[120] Lebecq, 'The Northern Seas'.

possibly expected to convert.[121] It has also been noted that Frankish kings probably provided role models for the seventh-century southern Anglo-Saxon rulers, who, in turn, may have aspired to gain for themselves the prestige associated with the Christian religion.[122]

With Christianity, monasticism also came to Anglo-Saxon England, as both the missionaries sent from Rome to Kent and the Irish ones active in Northumbria were monks. Although scholars have struggled to determine the exact type of monastic lives that they led, it would seem that their combination of contemplative and pastoral activities had a long-lasting impact on the history of the Anglo-Saxon church. Pope Gregory the Great's ideal of a mixed life of action and contemplation likely provided the main rationale both for the sending of monks as missionaries and for the lifestyle of the earliest religious communities in England.[123] This initial template can be seen to have influenced Bede's thinking on the organization of the church in the early eighth century and to have allowed, throughout the whole Anglo-Saxon period, for a certain blurring of the boundaries between communities of clerics with pastoral responsibilities and others devoted to a more secluded life of prayer.[124]

That English monks in the late seventh and eighth centuries were deeply involved in external pastoral activities is most vividly exemplified by those who, like Willibrord, Boniface and their disciples, left England to become missionaries on the continent. Most interesting, in this context, is the fact that Boniface's desire to take the Christian faith to the pagan Saxons appears to have been motivated by the perception that the latter were related to the English, as he wrote in a letter he sent to England in c.738.[125] The same sentiment can be found in Bede's *Historia ecclesiastica* with reference to the intention of Willibrord's teacher, Ecgbert, to preach 'the gospel to some of those nations who had not yet heard it', since 'he knew that there were very many peoples in *Germania* from whom the Angli and Saxons (*Angli uel Saxones*), who now live in Britain, derive their origin'.[126] In the event, Ecgbert's desire to become a missionary among the pagan Germanic peoples on the continent was frustrated, and he

---

[121] Yorke, *The Conversion of Britain*, 122–6. See also Higham, *The Convert Kings*, 82–90.

[122] Gameson, 'Augustine of Canterbury', 23.   [123] Foot, *Monastic Life*, 61–9.

[124] Thacker, 'Bede's Ideal of Reform'; Tinti, 'Benedictine Reform'; Jones, 'Minsters and Monasticism'.

[125] Boniface invited the English to pray for the mission to the Saxons, 'for they themselves are saying: "We are of one blood and one bone with you"': Tangl, ed., *Die Briefe des heiligen Bonifatius und Lullus*, no. 46, p. 75; Emerton, trans., *The Letters of Saint Boniface*, no. XXXVI, p. 53. See also Story, 'Charlemagne and the Anglo-Saxons', 197, and Yorke, 'Boniface's West Saxon Background', 40. On Boniface, his life, works and legacy see, most recently, Aaij and Godlove, eds., *A Companion to Boniface*.

[126] Colgrave and Mynors, eds. and trans., *Bede's Ecclesiastical History*, V.9, pp. 476–7.

established himself in Ireland instead, but Bede's report attests to the existence, in the first half of the eighth century, of a shared perception of common ethnic descent which would have played a significant role in motivating the Anglo-Saxons who wished to embark on missionary work. With time, however, it would seem that this sense of shared ethnicity faded, for the hagiographical texts which were written in the eighth and ninth centuries to celebrate the missionaries' lives and deaths do not refer to shared Germanic identity as a particularly significant factor in their decision to leave Britain and live a religious life on the continent. As James Palmer has shown, these texts point to a range of other elements, such as belonging to a family or a church, or being part of the same social network, as determining factors in the missionaries' and their followers' choices.[127]

The significance and impact of the insular missionaries' activities in the eastern Frankish regions went well beyond any possible initial desire prompted by a sense of shared ethnicity. It is important to bear in mind the political and ecclesiastical frameworks within which they operated, and the crucial support provided by the Frankish rulers who were extending or reinforcing their authority over the territories east of the river Rhine where the missionaries were active. Both Willibrord and Boniface sought papal permission before embarking on their preaching and reforming missions. They were consecrated bishops by Popes Sergius I in 695 and Gregory II in 722 respectively, so that they could (re-)organize the structure of the church in the regions where they were active. Recent research has demonstrated that most of the activities they carried out were in fact pastoral and organizational and often resulted in the foundation of new bishoprics and religious communities, rather than being strictly missionary or directed at pagans, with the exception of their work in Frisia and Saxony, which, unlike Thuringia or Bavaria, still hosted substantial pagan populations.[128] Monastic foundations, such as Willibrord's Echternach in modern Luxembourg or Boniface's Fulda on the border between Hesse and Thuringia, became important centres of cultural amalgamation through the merging of different traditions of monasticism, manuscript production and scribal and artistic training (see Map 1).[129] Scholars have identified several eighth- and ninth-century manuscripts produced at these and other foundations, such as the episcopal sees at Würzburg, Regensburg and Freising, in which the insular scripts imported by the Anglo-Saxons were used beside Caroline minuscule (see Figure 4), the

---

[127] Palmer, *Anglo-Saxons in a Frankish World*, 41–76.

[128] Wood, *The Missionary Life*, 57–99.

[129] Netzer, *Cultural Interplay in the Eighth Century*; Raaijmakers, *The Making of the Monastic Community of Fulda*, 175–264.

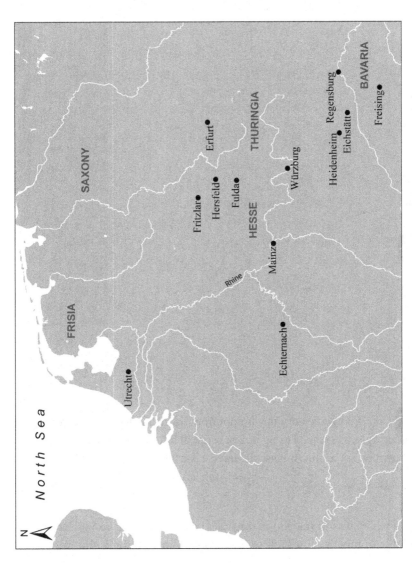

Map 1 The areas of activity of the Anglo-Saxon missionaries on the continent. Drawn by Erin McGowan

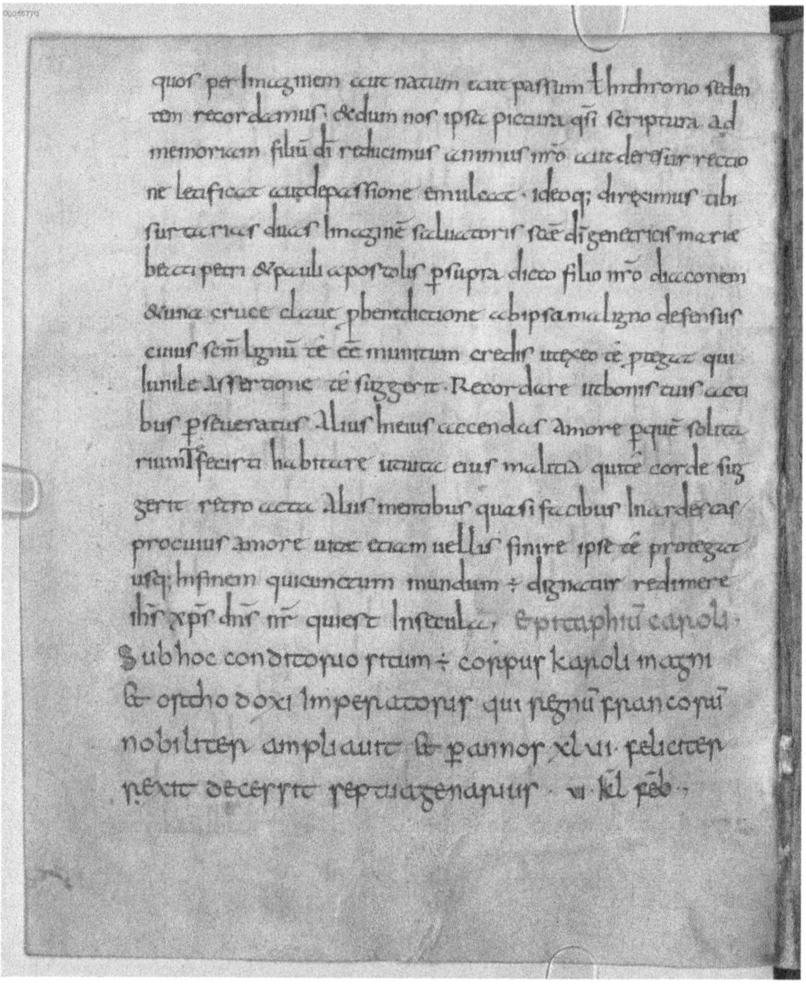

Figure 4 Ninth-century manuscript from Fulda in which the epitaph of
Charlemagne was copied using insular script; it follows immediately after other
texts written in Caroline minuscule. Bayerische Staatsbibliothek München, Clm
14641, fol. 31v

script which was developed in the Frankish realms in the second half of the
eighth century and which became ubiquitous during the reigns of
Charlemagne (768–814) and Louis the Pious (814–40).[130]

In fact, given the frequent movements of people and books throughout the
eighth century and beyond, also attested by the correspondences of Boniface

---

[130] McKitterick, 'Anglo-Saxon Missionaries in Germany'; Wieland, 'Anglo-Saxon Culture in Bavaria'.

and Lull (Boniface's disciple and successor as bishop of Mainz),[131] it is sometimes difficult to tell whether a manuscript containing insular script was made in England and then taken to the continent or produced in an eastern Frankish centre which employed Anglo-Saxon styles of script.[132] This was a time of extraordinary cultural interplay, in which the networks established by the English missionaries and their followers played a pivotal role.

To witness the resumption of such an intense movement of monks, books, texts and ideas between England and the continent, we have to move to the second half of the tenth century. At this point, however, the direction of the flow had changed, as Anglo-Saxon monasticism was now mostly on the receiving end.[133] To describe this period, scholars have traditionally used the phrase 'Benedictine reform' (due to the particular influence of the rule of St Benedict of Nursia), even though in recent years the term 'reform' has been repeatedly questioned and qualified, mainly because it cannot be found employed in contemporary sources.[134] Recent research has also highlighted the internal diversity of the Anglo-Saxon reform movement and has pointed out that the borders between reformed monastic communities and the more numerous secular ones were in fact less marked than the reformers' texts would have us believe.[135] What remains undisputed is the fact that many of the new ideas and ideals that can be found in those texts were imported from the continent. Two major figures of the movement – Dunstan and Oswald – spent time at continental monastic centres before being appointed to the most senior ecclesiastical positions in England, that is, as archbishops of Canterbury and York respectively. In the mid-950s Dunstan, who had been abbot of Glastonbury for about ten years, went into exile in Ghent (in modern Belgium) after falling out of favour with King Eadwig, and spent approximately two years in the monastery of St Peter, where he was able to observe the customs of a community which adhered to the Lotharingian reformed monasticism of Gerard of Brogne.[136] Dunstan's connections with Ghent and other Flemish religious houses were maintained throughout the later tenth century, as attested by the preservation of a group of letters written by the abbots of St Peter's at Ghent, Saint-Vaast at Arras and Saint-Bertin at Saint-Omer to successive archbishops

---

[131] For examples of books being requested and sent between Boniface and his correspondents see Emerton, trans., *The Letters of Saint Boniface*, nos. XIX, XXII, XXVI, LI, LIX, LX.

[132] For recent work on insular manuscripts on the continent (i.e. either made in England or Ireland and subsequently exported, or produced on the continent in insular style) see www2.le.ac.uk /projects/insularmss.

[133] Books and monks, however, travelled in both directions across the Channel in the second half of the tenth century; for an interesting recent case study see Weaver, 'Finding Consolation'.

[134] Barrow, 'Ideas and Applications of Reform'.   [135] Jones, 'Minsters and Monasticism'.

[136] Lapidge, 'Dunstan'.

of Canterbury between 980 and 991 (see Map 2).[137] The letters mention the frequent sending of messengers and embassies between Canterbury and the Flemish abbeys, as well as the archbishops' physical presence in Flanders, where they stopped when travelling to and from Rome to collect their pallium. Interestingly, these letters include requests for financial help and refer to earlier manifestations of generosity, especially from Dunstan, thus providing an important reminder that though the English reformers may have obtained much from their continental counterparts, especially in terms of spiritual connections, liturgical practices and monastic customs, they certainly reciprocated in a number of other significant ways.

Thanks to the mediation of his uncle Oda, archbishop of Canterbury (941–58), Oswald was sent to the important monastery of St Benedict at Fleury-sur-Loire, which hosted the remains of St Benedict of Nursia, or at least was believed to do so at the time.[138] According to Byrhtferth of Ramsey, who wrote a Life of Oswald shortly after his death in 992, Oswald spent an unspecified number of years at Fleury, perfecting his adherence to rigorous monastic life. Among those who followed Oswald was a man from Winchester named Germanus, who stayed behind after Oswald was summoned back to England and appointed to the bishopric of Worcester by King Edgar in 961 (which, from 972, he held in plurality with York until his death). Byrhtferth says that while at Fleury, Germanus 'sought to commit to memory the regular monastic customs',[139] and it was Germanus whom Oswald called back from Fleury to put in charge of the first reformed community that the bishop established in his diocese at Westbury-on-Trym. The monks of this new community lived at Westbury for about four years before moving to Ramsey (Huntingdonshire), a site which Oswald had acquired thanks to the generosity of Æthelwine, a local magnate and the future ealdorman of East Anglia.[140] Æthelwold, the third major ecclesiastical figure, who, together with (and even more than) Dunstan and Oswald is generally described as a main promoter of the English monastic reform, did not cross the Channel to spend time in a continental reformed monastery, but, while abbot of Abingdon, sent Osgar – one of the monks there and his future successor as abbot – to Fleury 'to learn . . .the way of life according to the Rule and to show it to his brothers when he taught them back at home'.[141]

[137] Brett, 'A Breton Pilgrim'; Vanderputten, 'Canterbury and Flanders'; Keynes, 'The Canterbury Letter-Book'.

[138] Nightingale, 'Oswald, Fleury and Continental Reform'. Oda himself had reportedly become a monk while visiting Fleury: Cubitt and Costambeys, 'Oda'.

[139] Lapidge, ed. and trans., *Byrhtferth of Ramsey: The Lives of St Oswald and St Ecgwine*, 'Life of St Oswald', III.7, pp. 66–7 ('regularia memoriter studuit scire instituta').

[140] Tinti, *Sustaining Belief*, 21–2.

[141] Lapidge and Winterbottom, ed. and trans., *Wulfstan of Winchester: The Life of St Æthelwold*, c. 14, pp. 26–7.

Map 2 Tenth-century reformed monastic communities mentioned in the text.
Drawn by Erin McGowan

Not only did Englishmen go abroad to learn about monastic customs and liturgical offices, but several continental monks also came to England over the same period. Most interestingly, monks from both Fleury and Ghent are acknowledged as having contributed to drawing up the *Regularis concordia*, that is the principal document of the English Benedictine reform, whose main authorship is ascribed to Æthelwold and which was meant to establish uniform observance of monastic customs throughout the country. The foreign monks' contribution is mentioned in the prologue of the text, which is said to incorporate 'their praiseworthy customs', through an explicit reference to the instructions that Pope Gregory the Great ('our holy patron') had given Augustine in the late sixth century, when he had told him that for 'the advancement of the young English church, he should establish therein the honorable customs of the churches of Gaul as well as those of Rome'.[142] Tenth-century imitation of continental monastic observance was thus compared with the mission sent by Gregory the Great and the recommendation – reported by Bede – that the pope made to Augustine to adopt 'any customs in the Roman or the Gaulish church or any other church which may be more pleasing to God'.[143] This passage sheds significant light on the reformers' initiatives; as Drew Jones has noted, their imitation of monastic customs from abroad was truly innovative,[144] but it was justified through recourse to the oldest and most venerable precedent of contacts with, and adoption of, continental practices.[145]

An eminent monk from Fleury who is known to have spent a couple of years in the English reformed monastery of Ramsey was Abbo, who shortly after his return from England went on to become abbot at Fleury. His arrival at Ramsey in 985 followed Archbishop Oswald's request for a teacher from the renowned continental foundation where Oswald himself had spent some formative years in the 950s. A number of surviving texts, written by Abbo and other scholars who had known him well, such as Byrhtferth, one of his students at Ramsey, and Aimoin, his biographer, allow for the reconstruction of a relatively detailed picture of Abbo's experience at Ramsey, where he apparently put on weight

[142] Translation adapted from Symons, ed. and trans., *Regularis concordia*, c. 5, p. 3 ('ut non solum Romanae uerum etiam Galliarum honestos aecclesiarum usus <in> rudi Anglorum ecclesia decorando constitueret').
[143] Colgrave and Mynors, eds. and trans., *Bede's Ecclesiastical History*, I.27, pp. 80–1.
[144] Jones, 'Minsters and Monasticism', 517.
[145] Reference to Gregory the Great and Augustine's time can also be found in another text probably written by Æthelwold and known as 'King Edgar's Establishment of the Monasteries'. In this case attention is drawn to the monasteries that Gregory had instructed Augustine to found so that their inmates could lead the same mode of life which the apostles maintained at the beginning of Christianity. The promotion of monastic life in Æthelwold's time emerges from this vernacular text as the restoration of an ideal past. See Jones, 'Ælfric and the Limits of "Benedictine Reform"', 72–3.

because of the foreign cooking and beer drinking.[146] Through close analysis of a letter that Abbo sent to Ramsey after returning to Fleury, a letter normally referred to as *Questiones grammaticales*, Roger Wright has deduced that Abbo's English students – whom he addressed as *Angligeni fratres* – were probably interested in speaking Latin and not just singing or reading it aloud. The nature of the numerous questions on pronunciation answered in this letter would also seem to indicate that Abbo and the English monks of Ramsey spoke Latin to each other; also, although Abbo had been exposed to both spoken and written Old English, there is no evidence that he was able to express himself in English.[147] Abbo's experience in England and the contents of this letter open an interesting window onto the nature of the many cross-Channel encounters that characterized the monastic revival of the second half of the tenth century.[148]

Exchanges and encounters with monks from West Frankish, Flemish and Lotharingian communities had significant influence on tenth-century Anglo-Saxon monasticism, but it should be borne in mind that fundamental sources of inspiration were also found in earlier, Carolingian precedents. This is particularly the case with the early ninth-century reforms of monastic and canonical life which were promoted at the councils of Aachen in 816 and 817. The decrees promulgated at these meetings imposed uniformity of monastic life and adherence to the Rule of St Benedict. This legislation, together with the version of the Rule which had originated in the wake of the Aachen reforms and the Frankish customaries that were written to adapt the original customs to ninth-century circumstances, enjoyed significant circulation in tenth- and eleventh-century England, as is attested by a number of manuscripts containing early recensions of these texts.[149] It has also been demonstrated that Æthelwold's Old English translation of the Rule shows awareness of the ninth-century Frankish adaptations,[150] and that the English reformers shared the Carolingians' aspirations to impose uniformity of liturgical practices and monastic customs. England is often said to have 'caught up' with the continent in the tenth century following the arrival of texts and ideas associated with earlier reforming efforts in the Carolingian Empire, but it is important to bear in mind that inspiration from earlier monastic texts and legislation can be recognized behind tenth-century reforming efforts both in England and on the continent. In fact, it has been observed that it is sometimes difficult to establish the extent to which a customary like the English *Regularis concordia* was indebted to continental

---

[146] Dachowsky, *First Among Abbots*, 69.   [147] Wright, 'Abbo of Fleury'.
[148] See further Mostert, 'Relations between Fleury and England'.
[149] Gretsch, 'Cambridge, Corpus Christi College 57'.
[150] Gretsch, *The Intellectual Foundations*, 255–9.

contemporary influence, such as that emanating from Fleury, since similarities may also be due to shared inspiration from older Carolingian traditions.[151]

What remains certain is that in the second half of the tenth century and beyond, religious leaders in England strived to rectify the lifestyle and liturgical practices of a number of monastic communities, such as those at Glastonbury, Abingdon, Winchester, Ramsey, Worcester and so on, with consequences which would impact society at large; in the process, continental examples of similar initiatives, both earlier and contemporary, were actively sought after as direct sources of inspiration. This is not to say that the outcomes were identical. Indeed, when opportunities for direct comparisons arose, differences were noted; these could range from aspects of Latin pronunciation, as was the case at Ramsey during and after Abbo's sojourn, to explicit criticism of monastic involvement in preaching to the laity, as attested in the Life of St Wulfstan of Worcester, written in Old English by Coleman shortly after the bishop's death in 1095, but only surviving in the Latin translation made by William of Malmesbury at some point between 1126 and *c.*1140. In an episode dating to the mid-eleventh century, when Wulfstan was prior at Worcester, a visiting monk from overseas – called Winrich – made it clear that he did not think it appropriate for Wulfstan to be involved in such pastoral activities, since in his experience preaching was not a monk's task.[152] Notwithstanding all the contacts that the English reformers had with communities on the continent, monastic participation in the delivery of pastoral care – which had characterized the Anglo-Saxon church from its early days – is attested throughout and beyond the tenth-century reform, thus distinguishing English monks from their colleagues overseas. This was especially evident at places like Worcester, Winchester, Canterbury and Sherborne, where monastic cathedral chapters (another distinctively Anglo-Saxon phenomenon) were established at a time when those towns were expanding and where members of the cathedral communities had plenty of opportunities to interact with the local population.[153]

7 Travel and Trade

At the heart of all relations between the Anglo-Saxons and the European continent there was travel in both directions. Travel took kings, ecclesiastics, diplomats, merchants, pilgrims and many others to the continent in person, and facilitated communication through correspondence. Even when travel

---

[151] Wormald, 'Æthelwold and His Continental Counterparts'; Nightingale, 'Oswald, Fleury and Continental Reform'.

[152] Winterbottom and Thomson, ed. and trans., *William of Malmesbury: Saints' Lives*, 'Life of Wulfstan', I.8, pp. 34–9.

[153] Tinti, 'Benedictine Reform'.

was not experienced in person, but reported, it would contribute to the shaping of ideas about distant places and peoples. Every early medieval journey between England and the continent would entail different forms of travel, covering both sea and land, but in the course of our period the logistics and practicalities of such journeys could vary notably and the choices that travellers made in terms of routes depended on a number of different factors. In the late sixth century, when the Frankish princess Bertha reached Kent to marry Æthelberht, and when Augustine and his companions landed on those same shores following their long trip from Rome, maritime connections between southern Britain and the continent were organized through ad hoc arrangements, as frequent communications had declined after the end of Roman domination. But it seems that shortly afterwards, that is, at the start of the seventh century, cross-Channel traffic began to pick up again, with ports appearing on both sides.[154] Connections between these sites, which in Latin sources are called *emporia, portus* or *vici*, became intense in the course of the seventh and eighth centuries and in some cases continued into the ninth and early tenth centuries.[155]

Written sources, excavations and coin finds have allowed scholars to identify shipping lanes as well as the commercial activities that took place at these *emporia* (see Map 3). Eastern and south-eastern ports, such as those at York, Ipswich and London, provided connections to Walcheren/Domburg and Dorestad (in the modern-day Netherlands); from there travellers could then reach Frisia, Austrasia and the Rhineland. South-eastern ports, like those at London and around Canterbury, had ships sailing to Quentovic on the river Canche, south of modern Boulogne, whereas from *Hamwic*, near modern Southampton, one could travel to Normandy and the Seine valley.[156] The earliest Life of St Boniface, written by Willibald shortly after his death, reveals that he left England from London both in 716 and in 718, but while in the former case he took a boat to Dorestad in order to reach Willibrord in Frisia, two years later he sailed to Quentovic to go to Rome.[157] According to what Stephen of Ripon wrote in his Life of Bishop Wilfrid, who went to Rome three times between the mid-seventh and the early eighth century, Quentovic provided the most direct route to the Eternal City at this time.[158] Theodore, who was sent

---

[154] Lebecq, 'England and the Continent'.   [155] Coupland, 'Trading Places'.

[156] Lebecq, 'England and the Continent', 59.   [157] Lebecq, 'England and the Continent', 58.

[158] Colgrave, ed. and trans., *The Life of Bishop Wilfrid*, c. 25, pp. 50–1. Though, of course, the choice of port at which to disembark would have depended on where one was leaving from: Willibald and Wynnebald, for instance, went from *Hamwic* to Rouen in 721; see below, text corresponding to n. 177.

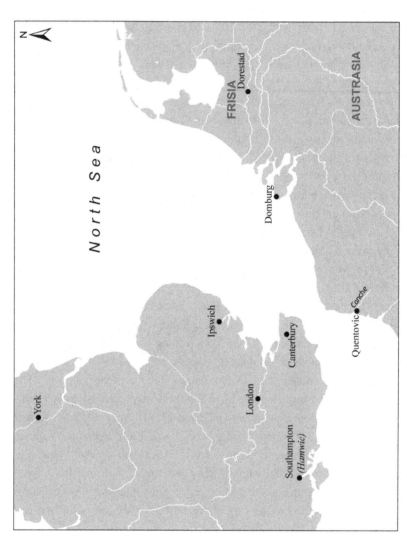

Map 3 Early medieval ports and trading centres on the North Sea and the Channel (seventh–ninth centuries). Drawn by Erin McGowan

from Rome to take up the Canterbury episcopal see in 668, also sailed from Quentovic to cross the Channel.[159]

All these ports were bustling centres of activity, where pilgrims would mix with merchants, sailors, artisans, toll collectors and moneyers. In *c.*730 Bede famously described London as an *emporium*, that is, a trading town 'for many nations who came to it by land and sea'.[160] Interestingly the location of the London *emporium*, or, as it was called in Old English, *Lundenwic*, was not in the old Roman city but more to the west, in the area of Covent Garden and the Strand, for easier access to the river Thames. Archaeological excavations have revealed commercial links with the Rhineland, northern France and the Low Countries, all regions that would have been reached from London through the shipping lanes described above.[161] It seems that the ships leaving from the Anglo-Saxon *emporia* took metals, salt, cloth and slaves to the continent, while those travelling in the opposite direction brought processed products, such as wine, millstones and weapons.[162] The intensity of the exchanges is reflected in the coinage, as the different polities where these ports were located stopped issuing gold coins in favour of silver at roughly the same time as one another, namely in the second half of the seventh century, with mints at London, Canterbury, Quentovic and Dorestad becoming particularly productive.[163] Rulers appointed officials, known as *procuratores* on the continent, who were in charge of collecting taxes from the merchants at these *emporia*, as well as other places such as Alpine passes. Tolls are known to have amounted to 10 per cent of the value of the goods carried by merchants at both Quentovic and Dorestad.

Thanks to the preservation of a letter that Charlemagne sent to King Offa of Mercia in 796, we know about a number of interesting aspects regarding the movement of people and goods between England and the Frankish territories at this time. Most revealing is the Frankish ruler's complaint about Anglo-Saxon merchants who masqueraded as pilgrims in order to avoid having to pay tolls at the appointed places.[164] The letter is part of an ongoing conversation between the two rulers, one in which pilgrims, merchants and goods feature prominently. Charlemagne wrote that pilgrims on their way to Rome were allowed to bring with them the things that they needed for their journey ('secum necessaria portantes'), but merchants had fraudulently tried to mingle with them to avoid taxation. The Frankish ruler acknowledged that on occasion merchants could be

---

[159] Colgrave and Mynors, eds. and trans., *Bede's Ecclesiastical History*, IV.1, pp. 332–3.

[160] Colgrave and Mynors, eds. and trans., *Bede's Ecclesiastical History*, II.3, pp. 142–3.

[161] Naismith, *Citadel of the Saxons*, 72–104.

[162] Lebecq and Gautier, 'Routeways between England and the Continent', 19.

[163] Lebecq, 'England and the Continent', 59.

[164] Dümmler, ed., *Alcuini sive Albini epistolae*, no. 100, p. 145; Whitelock, ed., *English Historical Documents*, no. 197.

victims of unlawful demands, something about which Offa had complained in an earlier letter, and he indicated that on those occasions they had the right to appeal to the king himself or to his judges. While on the topic, Charlemagne asked for reciprocity so that Frankish merchants could have the same treatment when travelling to Offa's territory.

International travellers needed written permissions or safe conducts to facilitate their journeys. That these were issued with frequency is confirmed by the preservation of a number of models for such texts in Frankish formularies, including a template for merchants and several examples of letters of introduction for pilgrims.[165] Models of this kind do not survive from Anglo-Saxon England, but narrative sources often refer to the letters of introduction that travellers were carrying.[166] These could also be acquired along the way, as was the case for Ceolfrith, abbot of the double monastery of Wearmouth and Jarrow in Northumbria: after reaching Gaul while on his way to Rome in 716, he was welcomed by King Chilperic II of Neustria, who gave him letters of introduction 'for all parts of his kingdom so that in all places he could be received in peace and nobody could delay his journey'.[167] The routes that Anglo-Saxon travellers took to reach their final destination on the continent (and, vice versa, the routes used to reach England by continental travellers) depended on several different factors and were obviously also shaped by the networks of people and institutions that they could rely upon for assistance and hospitality. That was the case from the very beginning of our period, as attested by the preservation of various letters that Gregory the Great wrote in 596 to rulers and ecclesiastics in Gaul, asking them to provide protection and assistance for Augustine and his companions on their way to Kent.[168]

Half a century later, the young Wilfrid was able to rely on various people and their respective social networks when undertaking his first trip to Rome, starting with Eanflæd, wife of King Oswiu of Northumbria, who, according to Bede, commended Wilfrid to her cousin King Eorcenberht of Kent by 'asking him to send Wilfrid honourably to Rome'.[169] Wilfrid had to wait for some time until

---

[165] Pelteret, 'Not All Roads', 26–8.

[166] A significant example is provided by the Life of St Boniface, who, upon his arrival in Rome in 718, was asked by Pope Gregory II if he had come with a letter of recommendation from his bishop, which Boniface was able to produce together with other letters: Levison, ed., *Vita Bonifatii*, c. 5, p. 21. For a translation of the Latin text see Talbot, trans., *Willibald: The Life of Saint Boniface*, 120–1. Evidence from the later Anglo-Saxon period points to the carrying of seals or sealed documents as a means through which legitimate travellers, that is, mainly merchants and pilgrims, could identify themselves abroad; see Benham, 'The Earliest Arbitration Treaty?'

[167] Grocock and Wood, ed. and trans., *Anonymous Life of Ceolfrith*, c. 32, pp. 112–13.

[168] Markus, *Gregory the Great*, pp. 177–87.

[169] Colgrave and Mynors, eds. and trans., *Bede's Ecclesiastical History*, V.19, pp. 518–19.

the king had found someone whom he could entrust with the task. This person was another young Northumbrian man, Benedict Biscop, with whom Wilfrid reached Lyons. At that point the two separated, possibly because of tensions between them, and Biscop carried on with his journey, while Wilfrid stayed behind for some time before finally reaching Rome, probably in 654.[170] In the course of his second trip to Rome in 679, Wilfrid was also given a guide in the person of Deodatus, bishop of Toul, by Dagobert II, king of Austrasia. In this case Wilfrid could rely on a different set of connections, thanks to the support of a ruler whom Wilfrid himself had previously helped return from exile in Ireland.[171] Stephen of Ripon, Wilfrid's biographer, reports that Deodatus took him south, across the Alps, to the court of Perctarit, king of the Lombards. Links between the latter and the Merovingians may have gone back to the time when, according to Paul the Deacon, Perctarit, himself an exile, spent some time in Gaul and had been about to cross the Channel to reach Britain when he received the news that it was now safe for him to go back to Lombardy.[172]

Wilfrid was exceptionally well connected, and his trips to Rome are probably not representative of what other, humbler pilgrims would have experienced when journeying from Britain across the European continent. Those who could not rely on the hospitality of kings and bishops could knock at the doors of monasteries, whose precincts would normally include a hospice for pilgrims.[173] As the provision of hospitality for such travellers featured among the routine activities of early medieval monasteries, the presence of pilgrims in monastic hospices is only recorded when something extraordinary, or particularly worth reporting, happened. That was the case in about 787 at the monastery of Montecassino in Italy, where a deaf and mute English pilgrim arrived with his companions while on his way from Rome to the shrine of St Michael at Monte Sant'Angelo sul Gargano, in Apulia. According to the Chronicle of Montecassino, while praying at the shrine of St Benedict in Montecassino, the man miraculously regained his speech and proved to be proficient both in his native language, that is in English, and in Latin.[174] While in Rome the same man and his companions would have been able to stay at the *schola Saxonum*, the English quarter in Rome, which, as mentioned above, provided hospitality for visiting fellow countrymen. It is possible that other cities along the well-trodden path between England and Rome developed similar institutions. We know for

---

[170] Pelteret, 'Travel between England and Italy', 248; Ó Carragáin and Thacker, 'Wilfrid in Rome', 217.

[171] Colgrave, ed. and trans., *The Life of Bishop Wilfrid*, c. 28, pp. 54–5.

[172] Wood, 'The Continental Journeys of Wilfrid and Biscop', pp. 207–8.

[173] Pelteret, 'Travel between England and Italy', 252.

[174] Hoffmann, ed., *Die Chronik von Montecassino*, I.13, pp. 48–9 ('non solum in lingua propria hoc est Anglica, sed etiam in Romana').

instance that in the second half of the ninth century, the northern Italian city of Pavia had a *xenodochium* (that is a hostel for foreigners and pilgrims) known as *Sancta Maria Britonum*, whose name suggests that it provided hospitality for travellers from Britain.[175] Pavia, capital of the Lombard kingdom, maintained its pre-eminence after the Carolingian conquest of Italy; it was on the main route to Rome and there is evidence for plenty of Anglo-Saxons stopping there.[176]

When hospitality was not available, early medieval travellers would camp, as was the case for Willibald and Wynnebald when they were travelling from England to Rome with their father in 721. According to the Life of St Willibald, written by an Anglo-Saxon nun of Heidenheim named Hugeburc who had heard from Willibald himself the account of his travels, after crossing the Channel from the port of *Hamwic*, the three men and their companions pitched their tents near the city of Rouen, where they rested for some days before continuing their journey.[177] Tents were valuable objects in the early Middle Ages; they could be employed as diplomatic gifts and they also feature in late Anglo-Saxon wills.[178] Camping, in other words, should not be interpreted as a cheap or poor solution for travellers who could not find hospitality. Difficulties, however, were certainly experienced by many. Long-distance travel was expensive, as Hugeburc indicates when mentioning that Willibald, his brother and father set out on their journey after gathering the money necessary ('sumpturis secum vitae stipendiis').[179] A century later, in 849, Lupus of Ferrières wrote to an Italian bishop telling him that he was about to embark on a trip to Rome but was worried that he did not have the Italian coinage that would be needed there.[180]

Anglo-Saxon male ecclesiastics seem to have been especially worried about the dangers that women would encounter when embarking on long-distance travel. In a famous letter sent to Archbishop Cuthbert of Canterbury in 747, Boniface, writing from the continent, told the archbishop to 'forbid matrons and veiled women to make these frequent journeys back and forth to Rome'. He added that many of them perished along the way, and few kept their virtue; in fact, according to Boniface, there were 'very few towns in Lombardy or Frankland or Gaul, where there is not a courtesan or a harlot of

---

[175] Keynes, 'Anglo-Saxon Entries', 105.

[176] On Pavia see Majocchi, *Pavia*. In a letter of 799 addressed to Charlemagne, Alcuin says that he had spent some days in Pavia on the way to Rome as a young man: Allott, *Alcuin of York*, no. 75, p. 91. A century later, in 888, Æthelswith, wife of King Burgred of Mercia, died in Pavia, after having probably accompanied her husband in exile when he was forced to leave England in 874; see Keynes, 'Anglo-Saxon Entries', 115. Later on, in the tenth century, Bishop Theodred of London bought two chasubles in Pavia; see below, text corresponding to n. 196.

[177] Holder-Egger, ed., *Vita Willibaldi*, c. 3, p. 91; Talbot, trans., *Huneberc of Heidenheim: The Hodoeporicon of Saint Willibald*, 149.

[178] Matthews, *The Road to Rome*, 25.   [179] Holder-Egger, ed., *Vita Willibaldi*, c. 3, p. 91.

[180] Coupland, 'The Coinage of Lothar I', 178.

English stock'.[181] Beyond Boniface's likely exaggeration, one should not underestimate the difficulties that early medieval travellers, both male and female, could encounter. Several of them fell ill and died in the course of their journeys across the continent: the above-mentioned father of Willibald and Wynnebald did not manage to reach Rome as originally planned, as he only made it as far as Lucca, where 'he was struck down almost at once by a severe bodily sickness' and, after a few days, passed away.[182] A few years earlier, in 716, the above-mentioned Ceolfrith, abbot of Wearmouth and Jarrow, while also on his way to Rome, fell ill and only managed to reach Langres in Burgundy, where he died. Bede's account of the event reveals that Ceolfrith's party consisted of about eighty companions; following his death, some of them decided to carry on with their journey, others preferred to return home to report the sad news of Ceolfrith's burial, while a third group, out of their devotion to their father-abbot, preferred to stay by his tomb, 'among people whose language they did not know'.[183] The singling out of communication difficulties between Ceolfrith's disciples and the people they were staying with at Langres is evocative of the profound sense of estrangement and alterity they would have experienced following their abbot's death in a foreign country. More generally, Bede's remark is an important reminder of the role played by issues of identity and belonging in early medieval long-distance travel.

Those who embarked on long journeys by land and/or waterways would encounter a range of different landscapes, climates, people, languages, habits and foods. In such circumstances, they would also have plenty of opportunities to reflect on what distinguished the practices of the people they encountered from their own ways of speaking, dressing, eating and so on. Helen Foxhall Forbes has recently made a compelling case in this regard with reference to the employment of runic script by the Anglo-Saxon pilgrims who inscribed their names on the walls of the above-mentioned shrine of Monte Sant'Angelo sul Gargano, dedicated to the archangel Michael. The 5 runic inscriptions left by English visitors stand out among the *c.*200 names which were written on the chapel's walls between the seventh and the first half of the ninth century in that they are the only ones not employing Roman letters. As the variations among the runic inscriptions point towards different inscribers, rather than a single one, the choice to employ runic – instead of Roman – script would seem to be

[181] Tangl, ed., *Die Briefe des heiligen Bonifatius und Lullus*, no. 78, p. 169; Emerton, trans., *The Letters of Saint Boniface*, no. LXII, p. 118. On the women in Boniface's circle see Yorke, 'Boniface's West Saxon Background', 34–6.

[182] Holder-Egger, ed., *Vita Willibaldi*, c. 3, p. 91; Talbot, trans., *Huneberc of Heidenheim: The Hodoeporicon of Saint Willibald*, 149.

[183] Grocock and Wood, eds. and trans., *Bede's History of the Abbots of Wearmouth and Jarrow*, c. 21, pp. 70–3.

deliberate and probably dictated by a sense of shared identity among the English pilgrims who reached this remote shrine.[184] Although it is not possible to establish a clear chronological succession for the inscriptions, one can hypothesize that the Anglo-Saxons who arrived at Monte Sant'Angelo after the first runic name (or first cluster of runic names) had been inscribed on the wall would have been able to identify with a writing system which was familiar to them (but not to many other visitors) and would have been driven to add their own name on the wall by making use of the same script. They would thus participate in the devout act performed by all the other pilgrims who wrote their name (or had their name written) at Monte Sant'Angelo, but would do so by making use of a script which they could directly associate with their own distinct identity and provenance.

Pilgrimage to the Gargano shrine appears to have stopped in the second half of the ninth century following a Saracen attack in 869, though it is worth noting that more than two centuries later, Ælfric, the famous Anglo-Saxon homilist, mentioned 'Garganus' in a sermon for the dedication of a church to St Michael, indicating that the shrine was still well known in England as a special place of devotion for the archangel.[185] Attacks such as that of 869 obviously played an important role in determining long-distance travellers' choice of routes and sites to visit, thus affecting well-established systems of communication. This was particularly the case with the viking incursions of the ninth century, which severely disrupted the communication system connecting the various *emporia* which faced the Channel and the North Sea, to the extent that such ports as *Hamwic*, Dorestad and Quentovic were eventually abandoned. The only trade centres that survived were those based in old Roman cities such as London, York or Rouen, but even in these cases it is possible to witness important changes. In London, for instance, the *wic* was abandoned in the first decades of the ninth century and all activities, including commercial ones, moved back into the relatively safe walls of the Roman city.[186] Later on in the tenth century severe disruptions were caused by the Saracens who had occupied the site of *Fraxinetum* (present-day La Garde-Freinet, on the Saint-Tropez peninsula), on the Mediterranean coast of modern France. It is probably from their base there that the Saracens perpetrated several attacks on the pilgrims who were scaling the Alps to reach Rome.[187] Flodoard of Reims refers to large numbers of

---

[184] Foxhall Forbes, 'Writing on the Wall', 201.

[185] Pelteret, 'Not All Roads', 34. Mount Gargano is also mentioned in the letter that King Cnut sent to England following his visit to Rome in 1027. See Section 8 below.

[186] Lebecq and Gautier, 'Routeways between England and the Continent', 23; Naismith, *Citadel of the Saxons*, 105–24.

[187] On Saracen attacks from *Fraxinetum* see Bruce, *Cluny*.

English people being killed by the Saracens in 921 and 923, whereas in 939 the victims included people of various origins; in the following year the same author mentions a group of *transmarini* (i.e. 'from across the sea' and therefore, most likely, Anglo-Saxon) and other people from Gaul who were returning from Rome, many of whom were also killed by the Saracens.[188]

What is perhaps most striking is that in spite of such recurring events, people from England and elsewhere were still eager to cross the Alps to reach Rome, as the Eternal City continued to be a main destination (probably, 'the' main destination) of long-distance travellers in the later Anglo-Saxon period. Although we lack detailed narrative accounts like those provided in earlier times by Bede, Stephen of Ripon and others, by exploring different sets of sources, both written and material, it is possible to appreciate that travelling from England to Rome was still a popular practice in the tenth and eleventh centuries. Charters, wills and other sources from this period refer to the efforts made to gather the money necessary for this expensive enterprise, as well as the measures taken to deal with the consequences of possible death along the way or in Rome itself. For instance, a document preserved within the archive of the episcopal see at Selsey records that in the first half of the tenth century, a certain Wiohstan, planning to go to Rome with his wife and son, sold four hides of land in Sussex to the bishop of Selsey in exchange for 2,000 pence and a horse.[189] Those of more limited means could rely on other forms of funding, as attested by the statutes of the Exeter gild, dating to the mid-tenth century, which established that every gild member had to provide five pence to help finance the journey of any other member wishing to go to Rome.[190] The relative frequency of will-making before embarking on journeys 'across the sea', as trips to Rome are sometimes described in these documents, attests to an awareness of the risks that such long-distance travel entailed.[191] Death in Rome itself was also a possibility. In the earlier period, kings such as Cædwalla and Ine of the West Saxons had left their kingdom to go to Rome and end their days there, whereas later on, in the second half of the ninth century, King Burgred of Mercia went to Rome after having been deposed by the vikings, and died there in 874; he was buried in the church of St Mary in the *schola Saxonum*.[192] A papal bull of Leo IX dated 1053 attests that in the mid-eleventh century the English people who resided in the *schola* or were visiting could still be buried within its precincts. This appears to have been a special concession, since

---

[188] Pelteret', 'Not All Roads', 29–32.
[189] Sawyer, *Anglo-Saxon Charters*, no. 1206; Kelly, ed., *Charters of Selsey*, no. 16.
[190] Whitelock, ed., *English Historical Documents*, no. 137.
[191] Tinti, 'The English Presence', 348.
[192] Tinti, 'The English Presence', 361. On the *schola Saxonum* see also Section 4 above.

at this time all foreigners and pilgrims dying in Rome were supposed to be buried in the church of San Salvatore in Terrione.[193]

It is not possible to identify the reasons why or the means through which the *schola Saxonum* managed to negotiate such a deal, even though it is probably safe to assume that the long tradition of English presence in Rome and generous donations to the papacy would have played a role. For the later Anglo-Saxon period, such practices become even more tangible thanks to the significance and scope of tenth-century numismatic evidence: between *c.*920 and *c.*970 Anglo-Saxon coin finds in Rome are more numerous than those of any other coinage and include such remarkable hoards as the one which was found in 1883 during the excavations of the House of the Vestal Virgins in the Roman Forum.[194] The Forum hoard, as this is normally referred to in English, consists of *c.*830 coins, the great majority of which were issued in England between the 880s and 940s and assembled at some point between 942 and 946, when Marinus II was pope. The latter was the intended recipient of this significant gift, as clearly indicated by a pair of silver hooked tags which were found with the coins and which bear the Latin inscription 'DOMNO MA/RINO PAPA[E]', that is 'to/for Lord Pope Marinus'.[195] The traveller who took this donation to Rome cannot be identified with certainty, but Bishop Theodred of London (909 x 926–951 x 953) is a likely candidate for three main reasons. First of all, he is known to have travelled across the continent, at least as far as Pavia, for his will, written between 942 and the date of his death (951 x 953), mentions two chasubles (one white and one yellow) which he had bought at Pavia. The timing of his journey to Italy is compatible with the deposition date of the Forum hoard. Secondly, the contents of the hoard itself show a strong connection with London, which is the best represented single mint-place, especially among the most recent coins in the hoard.[196] Furthermore, the Latin inscription on the hooked tags implies literacy as well as an expectation of direct contact with the pope, both suggestive of a person of high status, likely to be an ecclesiastic.

Pavia, on the main route between England and Rome, was a major commercial town in the tenth century, still retaining the central administrative role which it had enjoyed as capital of the *regnum Italiae*.[197] Theodred bought his two chasubles there, but many other Englishmen travelled to Pavia to sell their goods. An early eleventh-century compilation known as *Honorantie civitatis Papie*, in a section containing material probably dating to the start of the tenth century,[198] refers to the

---

[193] Tinti, 'The English Presence', 360–1.   [194] Naismith, 'Peter's Pence and Before'.

[195] Naismith and Tinti, *The Forum Hoard*, with photograph of the two hooked tags at p. 293.

[196] Naismith and Tinti, *The Forum Hoard*, 43–4.   [197] Majocchi, *Pavia*, 39–67.

[198] Brühl and Violante, ed., *Die 'Honorantie civitatis Papie'*, 19, 37, 83; Majocchi, *Pavia*, 69; Pelteret, 'Not All Roads', 32.

decima (i.e. the 10 per cent toll also attested in earlier times) which merchants coming across the mountain passes into Lombardy had to pay on all their merchandise to representatives of the royal treasury in Pavia. Most interestingly, the text refers to the rows which had arisen between the treasury officers and some Anglo-Saxon merchants when the latter were asked to open their sacks and trunks. The king of the Anglo-Saxons ('rex Anglorum et Saxonum'), whose identity is not specified, then negotiated a deal with the king of the Lombards, establishing that Anglo-Saxon merchants would no longer be subject to the payment of the *decima*; in return they would send to the royal treasury in Pavia

> every third year, fifty pounds of refined silver, two large, handsome grey-hounds, hairy or furred, in chains, with collars covered with gilded plates sealed or enameled with the arms of the king, two excellent embossed shields, two excellent lances, and two excellent swords wrought and tested. And to the master of the treasury ... two large coats of miniver and two pounds of refined silver.[199]

Even though it is not possible to establish when exactly the events here described took place, nor the identity of the kings involved,[200] the evidence provided by this source points towards the relative frequency with which Anglo-Saxon traders reached Pavia, in light of the fact that it was considered more convenient to send the money and goods described than paying the *decima*. Tolls, however, continued to be a source of problems for Anglo-Saxon travellers to Italy, as attested by the letter that Cnut sent to England following his journey to Rome in 1027 to attend the coronation of Emperor Conrad II. The king wrote that on this occasion he had spoken with the pope, the emperor and the princes gathered in the Eternal City about the need to 'concede fairer law and securer peace' to the people of his realm who travelled to Rome. He went on to specify that 'they should not be hindered by so many barriers along the road and vexed by unjust tolls'.[201]

Far from being a nuisance just for the Anglo-Saxons who travelled to the continent, tolls featured prominently among the requirements made on contin-ental merchants who reached England in the eleventh century, as attested by a legal tract known as IV Æthelred, which only survives in a twelfth-century Latin translation.[202] The first section of this text lists the tributes that were to be paid by ships coming into London carrying various types of goods, including cloth, timber, wine and fish. The text refers to merchants of diverse continental

---

[199] The translation is from Lopez and Raymond, trans., *Medieval Trade in the Mediterranean World*, 58.

[200] See Pelteret, *Slavery*, 75 for the hypothesis that the treaty may date from Alfred's reign.

[201] Treharne, *Living through Conquest*, 31. See also Section 8 below.

[202] Robertson, ed. and trans., *The Laws of the Kings of England*, 70–9, esp. pp. 72–3.

provenance and the respective tolls they had to pay; explicit mention is made of men from Rouen, Flanders, Ponthieu, Normandy and 'Francia', as well as others from towns in the Meuse valley (Huy, Liège and Nivelles). Upon reaching Billingsgate, the area by the Thames just downstream from London Bridge, foreign merchants were asked to display their goods for pre-emption, that is, for the king's right to purchase goods at a beneficial price. The tract specifies that Lotharingian merchants from the above-mentioned towns in the Meuse valley had to pay both toll and a sum called *ostensio*, which was probably a payment made to waive the king's right of pre-emption.[203] That merchants of different provenance were treated in different ways is confirmed by the fact that the 'men of the emperor', coming from Cologne or other towns in the Rhineland, were entitled to the same privileges as those enjoyed by English merchants. This text is not without difficulties, however, and its exact date and origin are not easy to pin down. It has recently been suggested that its first, relevant section should probably be dated to the early Norman period (*c.*1066–*c.*1100), also in light of its frequent employment of French terminology, though it is worth pointing out that archaeological findings dating from the reigns of Æthelred and Cnut widely confirm the nature and geographical reach of the trade attested in this legal tract.[204]

8 Warfare and Conquests

Warfare provided plenty of occasions for the inhabitants of Anglo-Saxon England to come into contact with people from the continent. In our period most foreign incursions and sustained attacks had Scandinavian origins, though the earliest recorded reactions to these events do not show much interest in the raiders' provenance. In the well-known letters that Alcuin sent to recipients in Northumbria after the viking attack on Lindisfarne in 793, his main focus was on the extraordinary natural events which had preceded the raids and the reasons why God's wrath was manifesting itself in that way.[205] At this stage, viking raiders were most commonly referred to in the Anglo-Saxon Chronicle as 'pagan' rather than through any ethnic or geographical descriptor. As time went on, however, attitudes changed and one can detect a growing awareness that Scandinavian incursions were also occurring on the continent, as shown by the detailed information on such attacks provided by the Chronicle, especially in the late ninth century, when the vikings' movements across the Channel are

---

[203] Middleton, 'Early Medieval Port Customs', 333; Lebecq and Gautier, 'Routeways between England and the Continent', 24–9, with useful map at p. 30.

[204] See Naismith, 'The Laws of London?' and Naismith, *Citadel of the Saxons*, 141–81.

[205] Whitelock, ed., *English Historical Documents*, nos. 193 and 194.

accounted for through reference to the outcomes of their raids on Frankish territories.[206]

The raids which in the ninth century had a major impact on north-west Europe mostly featured people coming from areas of modern Denmark and Norway, regions which are obviously part of the continent, but which, as Lesley Abrams has observed, are often considered as set apart from the rest of early medieval Europe, both by contemporary chroniclers and modern historians, at least up until the creation of centralized kingdoms and their conversion to Christianity.[207] The sources at our disposal only allow us to see the Scandinavian raiders through their victims' eyes, as there are no written accounts from the viking world before the eleventh century. Records from England have made it possible to establish that incursions intensified in the 840s and that Danish armies occasionally overwintered there in the 850s.[208] A significant step up in the attacks was recorded in 865 when the Chronicle begins to refer to a 'great army' (*micel here*); the succession of raids recorded from this time on had an unprecedented and transformative impact on the English political landscape, as the kingdoms of Northumbria, Mercia and East Anglia succumbed to the vikings. The entries which report their success in these regions (in 876, 877 and 880 respectively) also mention that they 'shared out the land', adding in the Northumbrian case that 'they proceeded to plough and to support themselves'.[209]

We know very little about the process through which former Scandinavian warriors settled down in these territories in the course of the late ninth and tenth centuries. Interpreting the evidence that does survive requires a range of diverse expertise, covering place names and other linguistic evidence, archaeological finds, coins, stone sculpture and written texts. For many years scholars have disagreed about the scale of Scandinavian settlement in England, with philologists arguing for mass migration in regions where place names of Norse origin are most attested, while archaeologists have noted that burial evidence does not allow one to identify the spreading of practices markedly different from those of the indigenous population.[210] More recently and thanks to the detailed analysis of metalwork findings in eastern and northern England, positions have shifted,

---

[206] Nelson, "'A King Across the Sea'", 46–7. Nelson notes that, conversely, Frankish horizons by this time had narrowed, as late ninth-century annals from these regions refer to the vikings only when they make an appearance there, without providing much contextual information on their provenance or movements.

[207] Abrams, 'Connections and Exchange'.

[208] For recent discussion and re-evaluation of the evidence for Scandinavian presence in England before the mid-ninth century see Downham, 'The Earliest Viking Activity'.

[209] Hadley, *The Vikings in England*, 1–15. The Chronicle also specifies that in Mercia they gave some land to Ceolwulf, who had been appointed king after Burgred's deposition.

[210] James, *Britain in the First Millennium*, 238–9.

with several archaeologists arguing for larger Scandinavian armies than previously assumed; these would have created major settlement disruption followed by a new Anglo-Scandinavian phase.[211] Such new findings are allowing scholars to say more about the Scandinavian settlement process, whereas earlier analyses tended to focus on the final outcomes of cultural assimilation, visible for instance in the coinage issued by Scandinavian rulers in England. These can be seen in places like York and elsewhere adapting their rule to that of the Anglo-Saxon kings, making use of literacy and relying on the support of the church, as well as minting coins.[212]

The absence from the English archaeological record of burials that can be recognized as distinctively Scandinavian has been interpreted as a sign of the speed with which the newcomers appear to have adopted Christianity, probably following the example of their leaders.[213] Scholars, however, have also made room for the possibility that Scandinavian burials may not have been as distinctive as traditionally assumed.[214] At the same time, significant Scandinavian influence has been identified in other manifestations of reciprocal acculturation, such as stone sculpture, place names and other linguistic evidence. New styles and iconographies related to Norse mythology show how such motifs could be accommodated into funerary sculpture. Interestingly, stone carving was hitherto scarcely known in Scandinavia: its flourishing in England provides yet another example of the hybrid culture which emerged following Scandinavian settlement.[215] Place-name evidence has been at the centre of the debate on the latter's impact and has also been employed to cast light on the interactions between settlers and the native population, especially in those cases in which English and Norse elements were combined to produce new toponyms, and when it is possible to witness Scandinavianization of Old English forms.[216] This evidence has played an important role in establishing that mutual intelligibility between migrants and natives (both speakers of Germanic, closely related languages) was most likely and must have facilitated the process of cultural assimilation which followed the Scandinavian settlement.[217]

Notwithstanding all the difficulties and uncertainties of trying to reconstruct such dynamics of reciprocal acculturation, it is important to point out in this context that the viking raids and subsequent settlement in England represent the

---

[211] Richards and Haldenby, 'The Scale and Impact of Viking Settlement'.

[212] Hadley, *The Vikings in England*, 28–80.

[213] For a detailed discussion and a useful distinction between official acceptance of Christianity and the slower process of conversion see Abrams, 'Conversion and Assimilation'.

[214] Hadley, *The Vikings in England*, 247.   [215] Hadley, *The Vikings in England*, 214–21.

[216] For a relatively recent summary of the debate see Ryan, 'Place-Names', 10–19 and bibliography there mentioned. For a more detailed discussion see Abrams and Parsons, 'Place-Names'.

[217] Townend, *Language and History*.

closest and most impactful interactions with people from the European continent that the Anglo-Saxons experienced. Their significance for present purposes is amplified by the fact that Scandinavian incursions and settlements took place across several different and widespread areas in the North Atlantic, Ireland, western Europe and the east, as well as Britain.[218] Many of the Scandinavians who settled in England had come via other regions on the continent; this can be appreciated through the evidence for moneyers with continental names provided by Anglo-Scandinavian coins issued from the 890s in East Anglia and in the East Midlands and, some time later, also at York. These suggest that the vikings brought Frankish moneyers from the continent to set up mints in England.[219] Further metalwork finds attest to other types of continental connections facilitated by viking movements across the Channel, as is probably the case for a ninth-century Carolingian trefoil mount found in Leicestershire, with holes indicating that it was affixed to a surface, possibly a book (see Figure 5).[220]

Not only did the viking conquest of several northern and eastern areas of England take a considerable number of migrants from Scandinavia to those regions, but because of their movements and raids across several other widespread territories, their settlement in England generated new forms of interaction with the continent.

Much still remains unknown about this process, which obviously would have evolved with time and would have been characterized by regional variation among the different areas of Scandinavian settlement. The process would have also been directly influenced by the military successes of the West Saxon kings who, in the late ninth and first decades of the tenth century, progressively brought under their control the eastern and northern regions conquered by vikings. Yet, several decades after the initial political unification achieved by King Æthelstan in 927, Anglo-Saxon law codes of the later tenth and eleventh centuries refer to distinctions between laws 'mid Denum' ('among the Danes') and 'mid Englum' ('among the English').[221] But can such distinctions be taken to indicate that the inhabitants of regions of earlier Scandinavian settlement were still perceived as different when these legal codes were issued? Most historians nowadays agree that on the basis of this evidence, earlier scholarship has far too often assumed the existence of a clear-cut Danelaw area and that it

---

[218] Abrams, 'Diaspora and Identity', 18.

[219] Smart, 'Scandinavians, Celts and Germans'; Hadley, *The Vikings in England*, 65. Conversely, it would appear that many of the vikings who settled in the Cotentin area of Normandy came via the British Isles: Cross, *Heirs of the Vikings*, 4.

[220] See for more information https://emidsvikings.ac.uk/items/carolingian-mount/.

[221] Abrams, 'Edward the Elder's Danelaw', 130.

Figure 5 Carolingian trefoil copper alloy mount found in Leicestershire
© Leicestershire County Council, CC BY 2.0

would have been possible to recognize people of Danish descent throughout the country.[222] Our understanding of ethnic identities has changed profoundly over the past few decades, with significant consequences for the interpretation of this period of English history. By recognizing that identities are not fixed in time but evolve and should be understood as social constructs rather than the result of biological descent, the evidence provided by the sources which refer to 'English' and 'Danish' laws has been recast within new interpretative frameworks. These also give due consideration to the fact that references to the laws of the 'Danes' appear most consistently in the legal codes penned by Archbishop Wulfstan during a period of renewed Scandinavian attacks, which, at this time, were clearly perceived as being conducted by Danish warriors. Wulfstan coined the term *Dena lagu* in the early eleventh century, during the reign of Æthelred, but used it more systematically in the law codes he produced after Cnut's conquest of 1016. As Matthew Innes has noted, Wulfstan was operating in a troubled period in which perceptions of differences between Danes and English would have been sharpened by the new threats the former were posing.[223]

---

[222] Reynolds, 'What Do We Mean', 406; Abrams, 'Edward the Elder's Danelaw', 133.
[223] Innes, 'Danelaw Identities', 77.

A new wave of Danish immigration followed Cnut's conquest, but Scandinavian migration is also likely to have taken place in the immediately preceding decades, as indicated by a famous charter of Æthelred dated 1004 in which the king complained of the Danes, 'who had sprung up in this island, sprouting like cockles among the wheat'.[224] The charter is here referring back to a decree ordering the killing of all such Danes; this can plausibly be linked to the event recorded in various versions of the Anglo-Saxon Chronicle under the year 1002 and generally referred to as the 'massacre of St Brice's Day'. The Chronicle says that the king ordered all the Danish men who were in England to be slain because 'he had been informed that they would treacherously deprive him of life, and then all his councillors, and possess this kingdom afterwards'. The event is best explained within the context of the Danish raids of the late tenth and early eleventh centuries rather than through any assumption that the massacre involved the descendants of the late ninth- and early tenth-century Scandinavian settlers.[225]

The differences between the two waves of Scandinavian influx into England are numerous. In the late eighth and ninth centuries, viking raiders were initially just interested in loot; hence their well-known 'attraction' to monasteries and their need to move quickly rather than engage in battle. In the late tenth and early eleventh centuries, plunder was still an attractive prospect, but we also witness more complex relationships between the leaders of the various Scandinavian warbands and the English ruling elite, with the former often being employed as mercenaries; their loyalty, however, could scarcely be trusted and the re-establishment of peace often necessitated the payment of substantial amounts of money, called *gafol* (i.e. tribute) in the Anglo-Saxon Chronicle.[226] Furthermore, while the earlier vikings were most commonly referred to as 'heathens' in contemporary English sources, without a clear indication of their ethnic identity or geographical origin, the raids of Æthelred's time are generally described as being perpetrated by Danish men, and on the occasions when they interrupted their attacks and decided to return home, they are said to 'return from this country to Denmark'.[227]

It is also important to bear in mind that the political situation back in Denmark played a significant role in shaping the sequence, nature and intent of the Danish attacks in England. Swein Forkbeard is first mentioned in the

---

[224] Williams, '"Cockles amongst the Wheat"', 1. See also van Houts, 'Intermarriage in Eleventh-Century England', 244–5 for evidence of followers of Cnut marrying wealthy English women, as well as cases in which intermarriage preceded conquest.

[225] Keynes, 'The Massacre of St Brice's Day'.

[226] Keynes, 'The Massacre of St Brice's Day', 38; Lund, 'Why Did Cnut Conquer England?'

[227] Whitelock, ed., *English Historical Documents*, no. 1, s.a. 1005.

Anglo-Saxon Chronicle as taking part in such raids in the early 990s and it is not clear what his position was in Denmark at that time, following his rebellion against his father, King Harald Bluetooth, in the 980s.[228] But when we find him again in England in 1003, he was certainly king of Denmark. Ten years later, Swein went back to England with his son Cnut, possibly, as has been suggested, because he could not ignore the power and influence that Thorkell the Tall was achieving: after having raided England with his army for three years, Thorkell had negotiated peace, received the payment of a record sum as tribute and entered the service of King Æthelred.[229] As is well known, Æthelred eventually had to flee to Normandy, and Swein became king but died shortly afterwards and could not be crowned in York as planned: he was instead buried there in 1014. At that point Cnut was elected king by his army, but the English preferred to recall Æthelred from Normandy, and Cnut returned to Denmark. He was back however not long after, and thanks to his victory at the battle of Ashingdon (Essex) and the death of Edmund Ironside, who had succeeded Æthelred and with whom Cnut had shared the rule of England for a short while, he became king of the whole country in 1016.[230]

In several ways these vikings were more 'European' than their ninth-century predecessors: not only did they now come from a centralized and consolidated kingdom, but they were also led by Christian kings, following Harald Bluetooth's acceptance of Christianity in the 960s.[231] This was still relatively recent, and Denmark lacked an ecclesiastical organization comparable to that of most other polities in western Europe. In fact, proper dioceses were only instituted in Cnut's time and at this stage their bishops were consecrated by the archbishop of Canterbury.[232] One could maintain that in the Anglo-Scandinavian world of the first half of the eleventh century, England made Denmark (and the other Scandinavian regions which came progressively under Cnut's control) more 'European', while the Danish conquest of England, in its turn, had major consequences for the latter's relations with other polities on the continent. Several scholars, especially in recent years, have commented on the 'hybrid' nature of eleventh-century England, describing it as 'wholly interconnected', both 'European and Scandinavian'.[233] This is in many ways the result of a shift away from legal and annalistic texts, traditionally favoured by historians, towards a more holistic approach embracing other types of surviving sources. As Charles Insley has recently shown, historians have tended to regard

---

[228] Keynes, 'Swein Forkbeard'.

[229] Bolton, *The Empire of Cnut*, 208–11; Lund, 'Why Did Cnut Conquer England?', 37.

[230] Lund, 'Why Did Cnut Conquer England?'

[231] Lawson, *Cnut*, 16; Gelting, 'The Kingdom of Denmark'; Abrams, 'Connections and Exchange'.

[232] Gelting, 'The Kingdom of Denmark', 83.   [233] Ashe, 'Preface', vii.

the conquest of 1016 as one of little consequence, to be spelled with a lower-case 'c', especially when compared with the Norman 'Conquest' of 1066. The legal codes authored by Archbishop Wulfstan for King Cnut have played a major role in furnishing an impression of institutional continuity, but if one moves away from strictly institutional aspects to try to reconstruct what Insley calls the 'atmosphere of politics', that is, the values and assumptions which characterized political actions, one is bound to encounter a significantly more multifaceted picture.[234]

Literary scholars have shown what can be learnt from the evidence provided by Old Norse skaldic poetry in honour of Cnut, which, as suggested by Matthew Townend, was most likely produced and performed in England, rather than in Scandinavia.[235] This poetry attests to a vibrant, multilingual court culture, its primary audience being the Danes based at Cnut's court. Although Old Norse and Old English, as mentioned above, were most likely mutually intelligible, skaldic poetry made use of demanding forms; in fact, it seems that it came into being as a mark of distinction, whose full meaning and intended associations were often only accessible to those initiated in this particular mode of literary composition and performance. Even more interestingly, Townend has shown how the skaldic poetry of Cnut's time provides access to readings of events which, like the battle of Ashingdon of 1016, led to the Danish conquest of England: by celebrating the king's Danish lineage and his displacement of the Anglo-Saxon kings, such readings clearly mirror the point of view of Cnut's Danish followers. Skaldic verse can be contrasted with other sources, such as the Anglo-Saxon Chronicle, which furnish the English perspective on the same events through reference to the destruction of all the nobility of England and the employment of what Townend describes as a 'mournful, elegiac approach'.[236] One of the main differences between the Danes at Cnut's court and the Scandinavians who had settled in England in the late ninth and early tenth centuries is that the formers' voice (and their language) can be heard much more clearly, and this voice attests to a distinct identity and interpretation of the past.

As Charles Insley has also noted, English history and identity became a rather contested space in the first decades of the eleventh century, but Cnut appears to have navigated successfully through possible tensions and compet-

---

[234] Insley, 'Why 1016 Matters'. On traditional interpretations of Cnut's conquest as comparatively 'trauma-less', see also Treharne, *Living through Conquest*, 9–12.

[235] Townend, 'Contextualizing the *Knútsdrápur*'.

[236] Townend, 'Cnut's Poets', 208–10. See also Treharne, *Living through Conquest*, 43–7 and Insley, 'Why 1016 Matters', 18.

ing identities.[237] This becomes particularly apparent in the letters that the king
addressed to the English people in 1020 and 1027, which provide particularly
illuminating instances of what Elaine Treharne has called 'pragmatic ethnicity', that is, an ability to blend in with different group allegiances in order to
promote ethnic unity.[238] In both cases Cnut refers to the presence of English
and Danes in England, thus acknowledging the existence of different identities, but also depicts himself as the provider of just laws, peace and protection for his people. In the second letter the message becomes more ambitious
because of the special circumstances in which the text was composed, following Cnut's journey to Rome to attend the imperial coronation of Conrad II. The
letter furnishes detailed information on the event and its participants, who are
described as 'all the princes of the peoples from Mount Gargano to the nearest
sea, who all both received me with honour and honoured me with precious
gifts'.[239] Cnut was keen to show how far he had gone, both physically and
metaphorically. No other king from England is recorded to have been in Rome
since Æthelwulf's journey in the mid-ninth century,[240] but it was the size and
nature of the event that Cnut wanted to publicize most. The wide-reaching
character of the gathering is conveyed through the geographical references
provided: Mount Gargano was probably the southernmost place in Europe to
be well known among the Anglo-Saxons, also considering its previous popu-
larity as a pilgrimage destination and its mention by Ælfric of Eynsham in
a sermon written a few decades before Cnut's journey; for its part, the 'nearest
sea' ('istud proximum mare') is to be interpreted as a reference to the rulers of
the territories facing Britain on the other side of the Channel. Thus, by
drawing an imaginary axis which cut through western Europe and connected
Cnut's realm to all the polities which – through their rulers – were also
represented at Conrad's imperial coronation in the Eternal City, Cnut could
boast a truly international profile among the most powerful rulers in Europe.
The few names he drops in the letter are those of the most eminent people
present at the event: the emperor himself, the pope and King Rudolf of
Burgundy. Interestingly, both Cnut and Rudolf are named in the *Deeds of*

---

[237] Insley, 'Why 1016 Matters', 19–21.

[238] Treharne, *Living through Conquest*, 17–43. Treharne provides modern English translations of
both letters as well as the original Old English text of the earlier one. For the text of the 1027
letter, which only survives in a Latin translation, even though it was likely also originally
written in Old English, see Darlington and McGurk, eds., *The Chronicle of John of Worcester*,
II, 512–18.

[239] Treharne, *Living through Conquest*, 30.

[240] Tinti, 'The English Presence'. Interestingly, this very concept is expressed by the skald Sigvatr
Þórðarson in a stanza of a eulogistic poem describing Cnut's trip to Rome, in which he says that
'few ring-givers [i.e. generous rulers] will have measured with their steps the route south':
Treharne, 'The Performance of Piety', 344.

Conrad II, written by Conrad's chaplain, Wipo, who also attended the coronation. Wipo reports that the two rulers played a role in the ceremony by accompanying the emperor to his chamber at the end of the divine office.[241] His account would thus appear to corroborate Cnut's claim regarding the honorific position he was granted at this event.

Scholars agree that Cnut's experience of Rome, the meetings he had there and the events in which he participated played an important role in the development of the new imperial image which he began to cultivate in the years that followed this journey. The royal style employed at the start of his letter of 1027 to the English people ('rex totius Angliae et Denemarcie et Norreganorum et partis Suanorum', that is 'king of all of England and Denmark and the Norwegians and parts of the Swedes') would seem to represent the earliest attested manifestation of his imperial aspirations, especially in light of the fact that at the time of writing he was not yet 'king of the Norwegians'.[242] Cnut had defeated them in battle, but his invasion of Norway properly began in 1028. Timothy Bolton has observed that the expansion of his domain into Norway was probably dictated by his desire for prestige in imitation of the way in which Otto I's lordship over several peoples had made him eligible for emperorship.[243] The famous representation of Cnut and his wife Emma in the *Liber vitae* of the New Minster at Winchester (British Library, Stowe 944, fol. 6r), dating to *c.*1031, provides further elements pointing towards imitation of Ottonian and Salian ruler portraits (see Figure 6). In particular, it has been noted that Cnut's crown is different from that worn by King Edgar in the latter's depiction in the New Minster Charter, which has been otherwise identified as the main inspiration for Cnut's portrait. One of the main differences can be found in the bar over the top of the crown, which, interestingly, is similar to that of a ceremonial crown known to have been worn by Conrad II himself.[244]

The inclusion of Queen Emma opposite Cnut in this illustration is probably even more significant. Ottonian and Salian portraits of ruler-couples are also

[241] Mommsen and Morrison, trans., *Imperial Lives and Letters of the Eleventh Century*, 79.

[242] Darlington and McGurk, eds., *The Chronicle of John of Worcester*, II, 512. That is, unless this passage of the letter was modified at some point between its original, presumably Old English, composition and its inclusion in the Chronicle of John of Worcester, which contains the earliest surviving version of the text.

[243] Bolton, *The Empire of Cnut*, 306.

[244] Gerchow, 'Prayers for King Cnut', 226–7; Bolton, *The Empire of Cnut*, 296. Similarities between the ruler portraits in the New Minster Charter and the *Liber vitae* have been observed by several scholars; see Gerchow, 'Prayers for King Cnut', 223 and Karkov, *The Ruler Portraits*, 123. For a detailed description and analysis of the representation of Cnut and Emma in this drawing see Owen-Crocker, 'Pomp, Piety, and Keeping the Woman in Her Place'. See also Naismith, 'Currency and Conquest', 88, for similarities between Cnut's crown in the *Liber vitae* and the crown adorning the king's bust in his earliest English coinage.

Figure 6 Queen Emma and King Cnut presenting a cross to the altar of New Minster, Winchester. London, British Library, Stowe 944, fol. 6r © The British Library Board

likely to have provided inspiration for the depiction of the royal pair in the act of placing a large cross on the New Minster altar, while receiving from the hand of two angels the heavenly reward of a crown and a veil respectively.[245] The portrayal of a queen in such a prominent position was unprecedented in England and must be considered here in light of the extent

---

[245] Gerchow, 'Prayers for King Cnut', 223–5.

to which Emma contributed to making Cnut's rule both more English and more European. As mentioned above, Emma, whom the English called Ælfgifu (as shown in the Stowe 944 image), was the daughter of Duke Richard I of Normandy, who died in 996, and the sister of his successor, Richard II, as well as the widow of King Æthelred. Scholars have pointed out Cnut's political acuity in marrying Emma shortly after his accession to the English throne, especially since her sons by Æthelred were living in Normandy as guests of Richard II: her role at Cnut's court provided continuity with the English past, but also helped to keep at bay possible threats from Normandy.[246] Of course, in the long run, as is well known, the close association of England with the Norman ruling family which characterized the last five or six decades of Anglo-Saxon history, would lead to the conquest of 1066;[247] yet, what is perhaps most remarkable is the way in which an earlier, different conquest, traditionally considered less significant, contributed to cementing Anglo-Norman links.

The warfare and conquests of the viking age as a whole played a fundamental role in the shaping of these relations. It should be borne in mind that the Norman polity in northern France traced its origins to another Scandinavian conquest and subsequent settlement; indeed, the ethnic label *Normanni* was an obvious attestation of viking ancestry, as the same word had been used in the ninth and tenth centuries to refer to Scandinavian raiders.[248] The political, social and cultural geography of north-west Europe underwent a profound transformation over this period. As Katherine Cross has recently pointed out, Scandinavian raids and subsequent settlements made western Christian people revisit their conceptual maps in order to make room for lands and peoples to the north. Furthermore, because of the widespread impact of those raids and settlements, the histories of Britain, Ireland, Denmark, Norway and many areas of the Frankish Empire became interlinked, and the ethnic identities of their respective ruling elites intermeshed. In a landscape dominated by conquests and following the political and ethnic reconfiguration of north-west Europe, eleventh-century England occupied an unprecedented central position.[249]

---

[246] For a detailed account of Emma's life and her evolving role on the English political scene see Stafford, *Queen Emma and Queen Edith*, 209–54. See also van Houts, 'Intermarriage in Eleventh-Century England' for a discussion of the evidence for (and significance of) exogamy following the conquests of 1016 and 1066.

[247] For an insightful comparative analysis of Cnut and William of Normandy – the two foreign conquerors of eleventh-century England – see van Houts, 'Cnut and William'.

[248] On the relative similarities between viking raiding and settlement in England and Normandy see Cross, *Heirs of the Vikings*, 11 and 16 for a discussion of the origins of the collective name *Normanni*.

[249] Cross, *Heirs of the Vikings*, 1–10. See also Section 3 above.

9 Conclusion

Anglo-Saxon relations with (and perceptions of) continental people and polities varied in direction and intensity over time. Contacts with Frankish kings played a major role from the late sixth to the mid-ninth century, as Merovingian and Carolingian rulers often provided models of kingship for Anglo-Saxon kings, even though they were rarely willing to be seen as on a par with their English counterparts. With time, however, thanks to the emergence of the West Saxon dynasty, the latter's military success against the vikings and the progressive disintegration of the Carolingian Empire, power dynamics shifted, as demonstrated by the efforts made in the early tenth century by the emerging Ottonian dynasty in eastern Francia to secure a marriage alliance with the West Saxon royal family. Of course, this was not the first time that the Anglo-Saxons had engaged with eastern Frankish territories; in the late seventh and eighth centuries several English missionaries had moved there and had played a major role in the (re-)organization of the Church in those regions, founding new monasteries and bishoprics and setting up a wide social network which facilitated the movement of books and people between these continental centres as well as with friends and relatives back in England. From the second half of the tenth century, however, contacts became more intense with territories closer to home, especially monasteries in northern France and Flanders, while renewed Scandinavian attacks, leading to the Danish conquest of 1016, made England a crucial player in the political reconfiguration of north-west Europe.

Inevitably, therefore, the Anglo-Saxons' relations with other regions in Europe changed over time, even though, as we have seen, some places remained constant references. Rome certainly did, and it is probably because of its continued influence and attraction that the representation of Italy on the above-mentioned Cotton map displays a notable amount of detailed knowledge. This can be observed both in the correct relative positioning of the Alps and the Apennines, and in the depiction of a comparatively large number of towns, with Rome being especially prominent thanks to its six turrets (see Figure 7). It is pertinent to note in this light that Cotton Tiberius B.v, the manuscript containing the map – produced at Canterbury in the second quarter of the eleventh century – also includes on fols 23v–24r the above-mentioned itinerary of Archbishop Sigeric, who went to Rome to collect his pallium in 990.[250] Most of the Italian towns on the map (Pavia, Luni, Lucca and Rome) are also mentioned in the itinerary, and their location in relation to each other and the mountain ranges is also correct. Rome is thus set within a topographical context which appears to

---

[250] Tinti, 'Anglo-Saxon Travellers', 173–5.

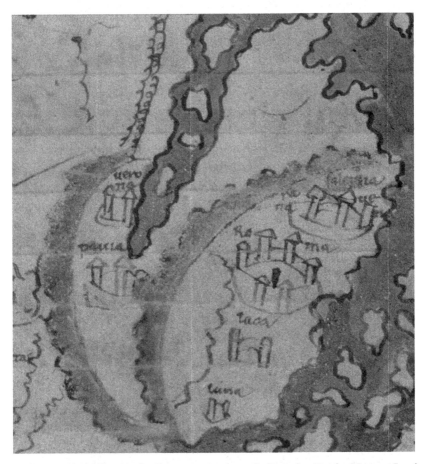

Figure 7 Italy in the Anglo-Saxon *mappa mundi*, featuring Pavia, Verona, Luni (*Luna*), Lucca (*Luca*), Rome (*Roma*), Ravenna (*Ravenana*) and Salerno (*Salerna*). London, British Library, Cotton Tiberius B.v, fol. 56v © The British Library Board

be anchored to the knowledge of travel to the Eternal City which had accumulated at Canterbury.

Just as the Anglo-Saxons' relations with and perceptions of most places and regions in Europe shifted with time, so did the view of England from the continent. We have looked in detail at the papacy's attitudes towards the English, starting with Gregory the Great's active interest in the late sixth century all the way down to Nicholas II denying the pallium to archbishop-elect Ealdred of York in the mid-eleventh century. We have also examined several instances of people from the continent taking the initiative to promote and cement links with the Anglo-Saxons: from Charlemagne's invitation to Alcuin to join his court to the correspondence of several late tenth-century abbots of Flemish religious houses with successive archbishops of Canterbury; from the legatine councils of 786 to the above-mentioned East Frankish promotion of a marriage alliance with the West Saxon royal family. But such waves of interest inevitably ebbed and flowed, and one is left with the overall impression that the Anglo-Saxons looked south more often than their contemporaries on the continent turned their minds to what went on beyond the Channel. When people on mainland Europe did so, they often looked or asked for money and other forms of wealth. This was the case for Pope Leo III, who in his letter of 798 to King Coenwulf of Mercia, reminded him of his predecessor's pledge to send 365 mancuses of gold to St Peter every year,[251] and for the above-mentioned Flemish abbots, who wrote to successive late tenth-century archbishops of Canterbury asking for financial help. And while there may be exaggeration in the description, provided in the *Encomium Emmae reginae*, of Cnut's generosity to the churches that he visited on his way to Rome,[252] coin finds in Italy and Rome attest to the importance of English payments and offerings in the early medieval European economy. These no doubt played a significant role in the reputation England enjoyed as a wealthy place in the eleventh and twelfth centuries.[253]

For their part, the Anglo-Saxons appear to have actively cultivated continuous interest in continental Europe. In spite of all the variations in intensity and geographical direction, one can appreciate throughout the period a persistent desire to emulate and/or establish close contacts with people and institutions on the continent. This is particularly evident in the seventh and eighth centuries, when the sense of inhabiting an island on the edges of the world still characterized the Anglo-Saxons' perception of their place in it, and it would seem to have acted as a factor in their attempts to establish relations with places and institutions that were perceived to lie geographically more centrally within the world. In the Viking Age, however, the situation changed dramatically, not just because of the enormous disruption that the raids caused both on the continent and in the insular world, as well as to the systems of connections between the two, but also because of the reshaping of international political allegiances that the Scandinavian incursions and settlement engendered. Eventually the position

---

[251] Naismith and Tinti, 'The Origins of Peter's Pence', 526–7.

[252] Treharne, 'The Performance of Piety', 347–51. Cf., however, the letter that Bishop Fulbert of Chartres sent to Cnut at some point between 1018 and 1020 to thank him for his recent gift and expressing surprise at learning that he was a Christian ruler: Behrends, ed., *The Letters and Poems of Fulbert of Chartres*, no. 37.

[253] See for instance the examples and discussion in Kaiser, 'Quêtes itinérantes'.

of the English kingdom in Europe became stronger thanks to these transformative processes, including after the Danish conquest of 1016.

When looking beyond institutions, kingdoms and other polities, we can appreciate that contacts with the continent were also pursued by Anglo-Saxons on a more personal level. Their experience varied depending on status, wealth, education and gender. Over time, men from the upper echelons of society generally emerge more clearly as participants in such relations. However, when one tries to go beyond the inevitable biases of the sources from our period, one can see that women could also play a pivotal role in England's relations with Europe. People from lower social classes could also find ways to travel across the continent, as was indeed the case for the tenth-century members of the Exeter gild who wished to embark on a journey to Rome. Notwithstanding the difficulties that could and did emerge while travelling such long distances and when reaching foreign destinations, the Anglo-Saxons actively cultivated their relations with Europe, and these had a major impact on the shaping of their economy, religion, culture and political life.

Appendix
Timeline

597: Augustine and his companions reach Kent from Rome

664: Synod of Whitby

669: Theodore becomes archbishop of Canterbury

678–9: Bishop Wilfrid travels to Rome to appeal to the pope against his expulsion from his Northumbrian see

695: Willibrord is consecrated bishop by Pope Sergius I

703–4: Wilfrid travels to Rome after being suspended from episcopal office

716: Abbot Ceolfrith of Wearmouth-Jarrow dies in Langres, on his way to Rome

721: Willbald and Wynnebald leave England with their father to go to Rome

722: Boniface meets Pope Gregory II and is consecrated bishop

731: Bede completes his *Ecclesiastical History of the English People*

754: Death of Boniface

757: Offa becomes king of the Mercians

786: Papal legates are sent to England

796: Death of King Offa, followed shortly afterwards by that of his son, Ecgfrith – Coenwulf becomes king of the Mercians

800: Charlemagne's coronation in Rome

814: Death of Charlemagne

853: Papal anointment of Alfred in Rome as a child

855: King Æthelwulf of the West Saxons makes generous donations in Rome

856: King Æthelwulf of the West Saxons marries Judith, daughter of Charles the Bald

865: An invading Scandinavian 'great army' is recorded in the Anglo-Saxon Chronicle for the first time

871: Alfred becomes king of the West Saxons

874: Death of Burgred, king of the Mercians, in Rome

899: Death of King Alfred

929: Bishop Cenwald's diplomatic mission to Germany to accompany King Æthelstan's half-sisters

939: Death of King Æthelstan

960: Dunstan is appointed archbishop of Canterbury

961: Oswald is appointed bishop of Worcester

963: Æthelwold is appointed bishop of Winchester

*c.*973: *Regularis concordia* is sanctioned at a council at Winchester

975: Death of King Edgar

978: Æthelred II becomes king of the English

985: Abbo of Fleury arrives at Ramsey

990: Archbishop Sigeric's journey to Rome

1002: Massacre of St Brice's Day

1016: Cnut's conquest of England

1017: King Cnut marries Emma, widow of Æthelred II

1027: King Cnut is in Rome to attend the coronation of Emperor Conrad II

1042: Edward the Confessor becomes king of England

1061: English mission to Rome led by Earl Tostig

Bibliography

Primary Sources

Allott, Stephen (1974). *Alcuin of York, c. A.D. 732 to 804: His Life and Letters*. York: William Sessions.

Arndt, W., ed. (1887). *Vita Alcuini*. Monumenta Germaniae Historica: Scriptores 15.1. Hanover: Hahn, 182–97.

Behrends, Frederick, ed. (1976). *The Letters and Poems of Fulbert of Chartres*. Oxford: Clarendon Press.

Bethmann, L. and G. Waitz, eds. (1878). *Pauli Historia Langobardorum*. Monumenta Germaniae Historica: Scriptores rerum Langobardicarum et Italicarum 1. Hanover: Hahn, 12–187.

Brühl, Carlrichard and Cinzio Violante, eds. (1983). *Die 'Honorantie civitatis Papie'. Transkription, Edition, Kommentar*. Cologne: Böhlau Verlag.

Colgrave, Beltram, ed. and trans. (1927). *The Life of Bishop Wilfrid by Eddius Stephanus*. Cambridge: Cambridge University Press.

Colgrave, Bertram, and R. A. B. Mynors, eds. and trans. (1969). *Bede's Ecclesiastical History of the English People*. Oxford: Clarendon Press.

Darlington, R. R. and P. McGurk, eds. (1995). *The Chronicle of John of Worcester*, II: *The Annals from 450 to 1066*. Oxford: Clarendon Press.

Davis, Raymond, trans. (1995). *The Lives of the Ninth-Century Popes (Liber Pontificalis)*. Liverpool: Liverpool University Press.

Duchesne, Louis, ed. (1955–7). *Le 'Liber Pontificalis': texte, introduction et commentaire*. 3 vols. 2nd ed. Paris: Boccard,

Dümmler, Ernst, ed. (1895). *Alcuini sive Albini epistolae*. In *Epistolae Karolini aevi*, II, ed. Ernst Dümmler. Monumenta Germaniae Historica: Epistolae. Berlin: Weidmann,1–481.

(1895). *Epistolae variorum Carolo Magno regnante scriptae*. In *Epistolae Karolini aevi*, II, ed. Ernst Dümmler. Monumenta Germaniae Historica: Epistolae. Berlin: Weidmann, 494–567.

Emerton, Ephraim, trans. (2000). *The Letters of Saint Boniface*. New York, NY: Columbia University Press (new ed. with an introduction by Thomas F. X. Noble).

Foulke, William Dudley, trans. (1974). *Paul the Deacon: History of the Lombards*, ed. Edward Peters. Philadelphia: University of Pennsylvania Press.

Godden, Malcolm R., ed. and trans. (2016). *The Old English History of the World: An Anglo-Saxon Rewriting of Orosius*. Cambridge, MA: Harvard University Press.

Grocock, Christopher and I. N. Wood, eds. and trans. (2013). *Abbots of Wearmouth and Jarrow: Bede's Homily i. 13 on Benedict Biscop; Bede's History of the Abbots of Wearmouth and Jarrow; The Anonymous Life of Ceolfrith; Bede's Letter to Ecgbert, Bishop of York*. Oxford: Clarendon Press.

Gundlach, W., ed. (1892). *Columbae sive Columbani epistolae*. In *Epistolae Merowingici et Karolini aevi*, I, ed. Ernst Dümmler. Monumenta Germaniae Historica: Epistolae. Berlin: Weidmann, 154–90.

Hirsch, Paul and H. E. Lohmann, eds. (1935). *Die Sachsengeschichte des Widukind von Korvei*. In Monumenta Germaniae Historica: Scriptores rerum Germanicarum 60. Hanover: Hahn.

Hoffmann, Hartmut, ed. (1980). *Die Chronik von Montecassino*. In Monumenta Germaniae Historica: Scriptores 34. Hanover: Hahn.

Holder-Egger, O., ed. (1887). *Vita Willibaldi episcopi Eichstetensis*. Monumenta Germaniae Historica: Scriptores 15.1. Hanover: Hahn.

Kelly, S. E., ed. (1998). *Charters of Selsey*. In Anglo-Saxon Charters VI. Oxford: Oxford University Press.

Lapidge, Michael, ed. and trans. (2009). *Byrhtferth of Ramsey: The Lives of St Oswald and St Ecgwine*. Oxford: Clarendon Press.

Lapidge, Michael and Michael Winterbottom, eds. and trans. (1991). *Wulfstan of Winchester: The Life of St Æthelwold*. Oxford: Clarendon Press.

Levison, Wilhelm, ed. (1905). *Vita Bonifatii auctore Willibaldo*. In *Vitae sancti Bonifatii archiepiscopi Moguntini*, ed. Wilhelm Levison. Monumenta Germaniae Historica: Scriptores rerum Germanicarum 57. Hanover: Hahn, 1–57.

Liebermann, Felix, ed. (1903–16). *Die Gesetze der Angelsachsen*. 3 vols. Halle: Niemeyer.

Lopez, Robert S. and Irving W. Raymond, trans. (2001). *Medieval Trade in the Mediterranean World: Illustrative Documents*. New York, NY: Columbia University Press (first published in 1955).

Love, Rosalind C., ed. and trans. (1996). *Three Eleventh-Century Anglo-Latin Saints' Lives: Vita S. Birini, Vita et miracula S. Kenelmi, and Vita S. Rumwoldi*. Oxford: Clarendon Press.

Mommsen, Theodor E. and Karl F. Morrison, trans. (2000). *Imperial Lives and Letters of the Eleventh Century*, ed. Robert L. Benson. New York, NY: Columbia University Press.

Robertson, A. J., ed. and trans. (1925). *The Laws of the Kings of England from Edmund to Henry I*. Cambridge: Cambridge University Press.

Symons, Thomas, ed. and trans. (1953). *Regularis concordia Anglicae natio-nis monachorum sanctimonialiumque*. London: Thomas Nelson and Sons.

Talbot, C. H., trans. (1995). *Huneberc of Heidenheim: The Hodoeporicon of Saint Willibald*. In *Soldiers of Christ: Saints and Saints' Lives from Late Antiquity and the Early Middle Ages*, ed. Thomas F. X. Noble and Thomas Head. University Park: Pennsylvania State University Press, 141–64.

Talbot, C. H., trans. (1995). *Willibald: The Life of Saint Boniface*. In *Soldiers of Christ: Saints and Saints' Lives from Late Antiquity and the Early Middle Ages*, ed. Thomas F. X. Noble and Thomas Head. University Park: Pennsylvania State University Press, 107–40.

Tangl, Michael, ed. (1916). *Die Briefe des heiligen Bonifatius und Lullus*. Monumenta Germaniae Historica: Epistolae Selectae 1. Berlin: Weidemann.

Wallis, Faith, trans. (1999). *Bede: The Reckoning of Time*. Liverpool: Liverpool University Press.

Whitelock, Dorothy, ed. (1979). *English Historical Documents*, I: *c. 500–1042*. 2nd ed. London: Eyre Methuen.

Winterbottom, M. and R. M. Thomson, eds. and trans. (2002). *William of Malmesbury: Saints' Lives. Lives of SS. Wulfstan, Dunstan, Patrick, Benignus and Indract*. Oxford: Clarendon Press.

Secondary Sources

Aaij, Michael and Shannon Godlove, eds.(2020). *A Companion to Boniface*. Leiden: Brill.

Abrams, Lesley (2000). 'Conversion and Assimilation'. In Dawn M. Hadley and Julian D. Richards, eds., *Cultures in Contact: Scandinavian Settlement in England in the Ninth and Tenth Centuries*. Turnhout: Brepols, 135–53.

(2001). 'Edward the Elder's Danelaw'. In N. J. Higham and D. H. Hill, eds., *Edward the Elder 899–924*. London: Routledge, 128–43.

(2012). 'Diaspora and Identity in the Viking Age'. *Early Medieval Europe* 20: 17–38.

(2016). 'Connections and Exchange in the Viking World'. In Fedir Androshchuk, Jonathan Shepard and Monica White, eds., *Byzantium and the Viking World*. Uppsala: Uppsala Universitet, 37–52.

Abrams, Lesley and David N. Parsons. (2004). 'Place-Names and the History of Scandinavian Settlement in England'. In John Hines, Alan Lane and Mark Redknap, eds., *Land, Sea and Home: Proceedings of a Conference on Viking-period Settlement, at Cardiff, July 2001.* Leeds: Maney, 379–431.

Abulafia, David (2015). 'Britain: Apart from or a Part of Europe?' *History Today*, 11 May. www.historytoday.com/britain-apart-or-part-europe.

Allport, Ben. (2020). 'Home Thoughts of Abroad: Ohthere's Voyage in Its Anglo-Saxon Context'. *Early Medieval Europe* 28: 256–88.

Appleton, Helen (2018). 'The Northern World of the Anglo-Saxon *mappa mundi*'. *Anglo-Saxon England* 47: 275–305.

Ashe, Laura (2020). 'Preface'. In Laura Ashe and Emily Joan Ward, eds., *Conquests in Eleventh-Century England: 1016, 1066*. Woodbridge: Boydell, vii–viii.

Barrow, Julia (2008). 'Ideas and Applications of Reform'. In Thomas F. X. Noble and Julia M. H. Smith, eds., *The Cambridge History of Christianity, III, Early Medieval Christianities, c.600–c.1100*. Cambridge: Cambridge University Press, 345–62.

Bately, Janet M. (2015). 'The Old English *Orosius*'. In Nicole Guenther Discenza and Paul E. Szarmach, eds., *A Companion to Alfred the Great*. Leiden: Brill, 113–42.

Benham, Jenny (2020). 'The Earliest Arbitration Treaty? A Reassessment of the Anglo-Norman Treaty of 991'. *Historical Research* 93: 189–204.

Bolton, Timothy. (2009). *The Empire of Cnut the Great: Conquest and the Consolidation of Power in Northern Europe in the Early Eleventh Century*. Leiden: Brill.

Brett, Caroline (1991). 'A Breton Pilgrim in England in the Reign of King Æthelstan'. In Gillian Jondorf and D. N. Dumville, eds., *France and the British Isles in the Middle Ages and Renaissance: Essays by Members of Girton College, Cambridge in Memory of Ruth Morgan*. Woodbridge: Boydell, 43–70.

Brookes, Stuart (2007). *Economics and Social Change in Anglo-Saxon Kent AD 400–900: Landscapes, Communities and Exchange*. Oxford: Archaeopress.

Brooks, Nicholas (1984). *The Early History of the Church of Canterbury: Christ Church from 597 to 1066*. London: Leicester University Press.

(2002). 'Canterbury and Rome: The Limits and Myth of *Romanitas*'. *Settimane del Centro italiano di studi sull'alto Medioevo* 49: 797–829.

Bruce, Scott G. (2015). *Cluny and the Muslims of La Garde-Freinet*. Ithaca, NY: Cornell University Press.

Campbell, James, ed. (1982). *The Anglo-Saxons*. Oxford: Phaidon.

Corning, Caitlin (2006). *The Celtic and Roman Traditions: Conflict and Consensus in the Early Medieval Church*. New York: Palgrave.

Coupland, Simon (2001). 'The Coinage of Lothar I (840–855)'. *Numismatic Chronicle* 161: 157–98.

(2002). 'Trading Places: Quentovic and Dorestad Reassessed'. *Early Medieval Europe* 11: 209–32.

Cross, Katherine (2018). *Heirs of the Vikings: History and Identity in Normandy and England, c.950–c.1015*. Woodbridge: York Medieval Press.

Cubitt, Catherine (1995). *Anglo-Saxon Church Councils c.650–c.850*. London: Leicester University Press.

Cubitt, Catherine and Marios Costambeys (2004). 'Oda'. *Oxford Dictionary of National Biography*. Oxford: Oxford University Press: www.oxforddnb.com/.

Dachowsky, Elizabeth (2008). *First Among Abbots: The Career of Abbo of Fleury*. Washington, DC: Catholic University of America Press.

Dailey, E. T. (2015). 'To Choose One Easter from Three: Oswiu's Decision and the Northumbrian Synod of AD 664', *Peritia* 26: 47–64.

Delogu, Paolo (1988). 'The Rebirth of Rome in the 8th and 9th Centuries'. In Richard Hodges and Brian Hobley, eds., *The Rebirth of Towns in the West, AD 700–1050*, CBA Research Report 68. London: Council for British Archaeology: 32–42.

Discenza, Nicole Guenther (2017). *Inhabited Spaces: Anglo-Saxon Constructions of Place*. Toronto: University of Toronto Press.

Downham, Clare (2017). 'The Earliest Viking Activity in England?' *The English Historical Review* 132: 1–12.

Foot, Sarah (2006). *Monastic Life in Anglo-Saxon England, c. 600–900*. Cambridge: Cambridge University Press.

(2011). *Æthelstan: The First King of England*. New Haven, CT: Yale University Press.

Foxhall Forbes, Helen (2019). 'Writing on the Wall: Anglo-Saxons at Monte Sant'Angelo sul Gargano (Puglia) and the Spiritual Significance of Graffiti'. *Journal of Late Antiquity* 12: 169–210.

Fruscione, Daniela (2010). 'Liebermann's Intellectual Milieu'. In Stefan Jurasinski, Lisi Oliver and Andrew Rabin, eds., *English Law Before Magna Carta: Felix Liebermann and Die Gesetze der Angelsachsen*. Leiden: Brill, 15–26.

Gallagher, Robert (2017). 'Latin Acrostic Poetry in Anglo-Saxon England: Reassessing the Contribution of John the Old Saxon'. *Medium Ævum* 86: 249–74.

Gameson, Richard (1999). 'Augustine of Canterbury: Context and Achievement'. In Richard Gameson, ed., *St Augustine and the Conversion of England*. Stroud: Sutton Publishing, 1–40.

Garrison, Mary (1997). 'The English and the Irish at the Court of Charlemagne'. In P. L. Butzer, M. Kerner and W. Oberschelp, eds., *Karl der Grosse und sein Nachwirken: 1200 Jahre Kultur und Wissenschaft in Europa*, I: *Wissen und Weltbild*. Turnhout: Brepols, 97–123.

Geary, Patrick J. (1983). 'Ethnic Identity as a Situational Construct in the Early Middle Ages'. *Mitteilungen der Anthropologischen Gesellschaft in Wien* 113: 15–36.

Gelting, Michael H. (2007). 'The Kingdom of Denmark'. In Nora Berend, ed., *Christianization and the Rise of Christian Monarchy: Scandinavia, Central Europe and Rus' c. 900–1200*. Cambridge: Cambridge University Press, 73–120.

Gem, Richard (2013). '*Gabatae Saxiscae*: Saxon Bowls in the Churches of Rome in the Eighth and Ninth Centuries'. In Andrew Reynolds and Leslie Webster, eds., *Early Medieval Art and Archaeology in the Northern World: Studies in Honour of James Graham-Campbell*. Leiden: Brill, 87–110.

Gerchow, Jan. 'Prayers for King Cnut: The Liturgical Commemoration of a Conqueror'. In Carola Hicks, ed., *England in the Eleventh Century: Proceedings of the 1990 Harlaxton Symposium*. Stamford: Paul Watkins, 219–38.

Goodson, Caroline (2010). *The Rome of Pope Paschal I: Papal Power, Urban Renovation, Church Rebuilding and Relic Translation, 817–824*. Cambridge: Cambridge University Press.

Gretsch, Mechthild (1999). *The Intellectual Foundations of the English Benedictine Reform*. Cambridge: Cambridge University Press.

(2003). 'Cambridge, Corpus Christi College 57: A Witness to the Early Stages of the Benedictine Reform in England?' *Anglo-Saxon England* 32: 111–46.

Hadley, D. M. (2006). *The Vikings in England: Settlement, Society and Culture*. Manchester: Manchester University Press.

Halsall, Guy (2013). *Worlds of Arthur: Facts & Fiction of the Dark Ages*. Oxford: Oxford University Press.

Hendrix, Julian (2010). 'The Confraternity Books of St Gall and Their Early Liturgical Context'. *Revue bénédictine* 120: 295–320.

Higham, N. J. (1997). *The Convert Kings: Power and Religious Affiliation in Early Anglo-Saxon England*. Manchester: Manchester University Press.

van Houts, Elisabeth (2011). 'Intermarriage in Eleventh-Century England'. In David Crouch and Kathleen Thompson, eds., *Normandy and Its Neighbours, 900–1250: Essays for David Bates*. Turnhout: Brepols, 237–70.

(2020). 'Cnut and William: A Comparison'. In Laura Ashe and Emily Joan Ward, eds., *Conquests in Eleventh-Century England: 1016, 1066*. Woodbridge: Boydell, 65–84.

Howe, Nicholas (2008). *Writing the Map of Anglo-Saxon England: Essays in Cultural Geography*. New Haven, CT: Yale University Press.

Hunter Blair, Peter (1971). 'The Letters of Pope Boniface V and the Mission of Paulinus to Northumbria'. In Peter Clemoes and Kathleen Hughes, eds., *England Before the Conquest: Studies in Primary Sources Presented to Dorothy Whitelock*. Cambridge: Cambridge University Press, 5–13.

Innes, Matthew (2000). 'Danelaw Identities: Ethnicity, Regionalism and Political Allegiances'. In Dawn M. Hadley and Julian D. Richards, eds., *Cultures in Contact: Scandinavian Settlement in England in the Ninth and Tenth Centuries*. Turnhout: Brepols, 65–88.

Insley, Charles (2020). 'Why 1016 Matters; or, the Politics of Memory and Identity in Cnut's Kingdom'. In Laura Ashe and Emily Joan Ward, eds., *Conquests in Eleventh-Century England: 1016, 1066*. Woodbridge: Boydell, 3–22.

Isaïa, Marie-Céline (2008). 'L'empire carolingien, prefiguration de l'Europe: du projet historiographique au programme politique'. Lyons: CHM. https://halshs.archives-ouvertes.fr/halshs-00392828.

James, Edward (2001). *Britain in the First Millennium*. London: Arnold.

Jones, Christopher A. (1998). 'The Book of the Liturgy in Anglo-Saxon England'. *Speculum* 73: 659–702.

(2009). 'Ælfric and the Limits of "Benedictine Reform"'. In Hugh Magennis and Mary Swan, eds., *A Companion to Ælfric*. Leiden: Brill, 67–108.

(2018). 'An Edition of the Four Sermons Attributed to Candidus Witto'. *Anglo-Saxon England* 47: 7–67.

(2020) 'Minsters and Monasticism in Anglo-Saxon England'. In Alison I. Beach and Isabelle Cochelin, eds., *The Cambridge History of Medieval Monasticism in the Latin West*. Cambridge: Cambridge University Press, 502–18.

Kaiser, R. (1995). 'Quêtes itinérantes avec des reliques pour financer la construction des églises (XI-XIIe siècles)'. *Le Moyen Âge* 10, 205–25.

Karkov, Catherine E. (2004). *The Ruler Portraits of Anglo-Saxon England*. Woodbridge: Boydell.

Keynes, Simon (1985). 'King Athelstan's Books'. In Michael Lapidge and Helmut Gneuss, eds., *Learning and Literature in Anglo-Saxon England: Studies Presented to Peter Clemoes on the Occasion of His Sixty-Fifth Birthday*. Cambridge: Cambridge University Press, 143–201.

(1997). 'Anglo-Saxon Entries in the "Liber Vitae" of Brescia'. In Jane Roberts and Janet L. Nelson with Malcolm Godden, eds., *Alfred the Wise. Studies in Honour of Janet Bately on the Occasion of Her Sixty-Fifth Birthday*. Woodbridge: Boydell: 1997, 99–119.

(2000). 'England, c.900–1016'. In Timothy Reuter, ed., *The New Cambridge Medieval History, III, c.900–c.1024.* Cambridge: Cambridge University Press, 456–84.

(2007). 'The Massacre of St Brice's Day (13 November 1002)'. In Niels Lund, ed., *Beretning fra seksogtyvende tværfaglige vikingesymposium.* Højbjerg: Hikuin, 32–66.

(2014). 'Swein Forkbeard'. In Michael Lapidge, John Blair, Simon Keynes and Donald Scragg, eds., *The Wiley Blackwell Encyclopaedia of Anglo-Saxon England.* 2nd ed. Malden, MA: Wiley, 452–3.

(2021). 'The Canterbury Letter-Book'. In Claire Breay and Joanna Story, eds., *Manuscripts in the Anglo-Saxon Kingdoms: Cultures and Connections.* Dublin: Four Courts Press, 119–40.

Körntgen, Ludger, and Dominik Waßenhoven, eds. (2011). *Patterns of Episcopal Power: Bishops in Tenth and Eleventh Century Western Europe.* Berlin: de Gruyter.

Körntgen, Ludger, and Dominik Waßenhoven, eds. (2013). *Religion and Politics in the Middle Ages: England and Germany by Comparison.* Berlin: de Gruyter.

Lapidge, Michael (1981). 'Some Latin Poems as Evidence for the Reign of Athelstan'. *Anglo-Saxon England* 9: 61–98. Reprinted in Michael Lapidge (1988). *Anglo-Latin Literature 900–1600.* London: The Hambledon Press: no. 2.

Lapidge, Michael, ed. (1995). *Archbishop Theodore: Commemorative Studies on His Life and Influence.* Cambridge: Cambridge University Press.

(2014). 'Dunstan'. In Michael Lapidge, John Blair, Simon Keynes and Donald Scragg, eds., *The Wiley Blackwell Encyclopaedia of Anglo-Saxon England.* 2nd ed. Malden, MA: Wiley: 150–1.

Lawson, M. K. (1993). *Cnut: The Danes in England in the Early Eleventh Century.* London: Longman.

Lebecq, Stéphane (1999). 'England and the Continent in the Sixth and Seventh Centuries: The Question of Logistics'. In Richard Gameson, ed., *St Augustine and the Conversion of England.* Stroud: Sutton Publishing, 50–67.

(2005). 'The Northern Seas (Fifth to Eighth Century)'. In Paul Fouracre, ed., *The New Cambridge Medieval History, I, c.500–c.700.* Cambridge: Cambridge University Press, 639–59.

Lebecq, Stéphane and Alban Gautier (2010). 'Routeways between England and the Continent in the Tenth Century'. In David Rollason, Conrad Leyser and Hannah Williams, eds., *England and the Continent in the Tenth Century: Studies in Honour of Wilhelm Levison (1876–1947).* Turnhout: Brepols, 17–34.

Leneghan, Francis (2005). '*Translatio imperii*: The Old English Orosius and the Rise of Wessex'. *Anglia* 133: 656–705.

Levison, Wilhelm (1946). *England and the Continent in the Eighth Century: The Ford Lectures delivered in the University of Oxford in the Hilary Term 1943*. Oxford: Clarendon Press.

Leyser, Conrad (2010). 'Introduction: England and the Continent'. In David Rollason, Conrad Leyser and Hannah Williams, eds., *England and the Continent in the Tenth Century: Studies in Honour of Wilhelm Levison (1876–1947)*. Turnhout: Brepols, 1–13.

Leyser, Karl (1994). 'The Ottonians and Wessex'. In Karl Leyser, *Communications and Power in Medieval Europe: The Carolingian and Ottonian Centuries*, ed. Timothy Reuter. London: Hambledon, 73–104 (first published in German in 1983 in *Frühmittelalterliche Studien*).

Lund, Niels (2020) 'Why Did Cnut Conquer England?' In Laura Ashe and Emily Joan Ward, eds., *Conquests in Eleventh-Century England: 1016, 1066*. Woodbridge: Boydell, 23–40.

MacLean, Simon (2017). *Ottonian Queenship*. Oxford: Oxford University Press.

Majocchi, Piero (2008). *Pavia città regia*. Rome: Viella.

Markus, R. A. (1997). *Gregory the Great and His World*. Cambridge: Cambridge University Press.

Matthews, Stephen (2007). *The Road to Rome: Travel and Travellers between England and Italy in the Anglo-Saxon Centuries*. Oxford: Archaeopress.

McKitterick, Rosamond (1989). 'Anglo-Saxon Missionaries in Germany: Reflections on the Manuscript Evidence'. *Transactions of the Cambridge Bibliographical Society* 9: 291–329.

(1995). 'England and the Continent'. In Rosamond McKitterick, ed., *The New Cambridge Medieval History, II, c.700–c.900*. Cambridge: Cambridge University Press, 66–84.

(2004). *History and Memory in the Carolingian World*. Cambridge: Cambridge University Press.

(2008). *Charlemagne: The Formation of a European Identity*. Cambridge: Cambridge University Press.

(2020). *Rome and the Invention of the Papacy: The Liber Pontificalis*. Cambridge: Cambridge University Press.

Merrills, A. H. (2005). *History and Geography in Late Antiquity*. Cambridge: Cambridge University Press.

Middleton, Neil (2005). 'Early Medieval Port Customs, Tolls and Control on Foreign Trade'. *Early Medieval Europe* 13: 313–58.

Miller, Maureen C. (2014). *Clothing the Clergy: Virtue and Power in Medieval Europe, c. 800–1200*. Ithaca, NY: Cornell University Press.

Mostert, Marco (2010). 'Relations between Fleury and England'. In David Rollason, Conrad Leyser and Hannah Williams, eds., *England and the Continent in the Tenth Century: Studies in Honour of Wilhelm Levison (1876–1947)*. Turnhout: Brepols, 185–208.

Naismith, Rory (2014). 'Peter's Pence and Before: Numismatic Links between Anglo-Saxon England and Rome'. In Francesca Tinti, ed., *England and Rome in the Early Middle Ages: Pilgrimage, Art and Politics*. Turnhout: Brepols, 217–53.

(2019). *Citadel of the Saxons: The Rise of Early London*. London: I. B. Tauris.

(2019). 'The Laws of London? IV Æthelred in Context'. *The London Journal* 44: 1–16.

(2020). 'Currency and Conquest in Eleventh-Century England'. In Laura Ashe and Emily Joan Ward, eds., *Conquests in Eleventh-Century England: 1016, 1066*. Woodbridge: Boydell: 85–98.

(2021). *Early Medieval Britain c.500–1000*. Cambridge: Cambridge University Press.

Naismith, Rory, and Francesca Tinti (2016). *The Forum Hoard of Anglo-Saxon Coins*. Bollettino di Numismatica 55–6. Rome: Istituto Poligrafico e Zecca dello Stato. Available online at www.numismaticadellostato.it/web/pns/bollettino.

(2019). 'The Origins of Peter's Pence'. *The English Historical Review* 134: 521–52.

Nelson, Janet L. (1986). '"A King Across the Sea": Alfred in Continental Perspective'. *Transactions of the Royal Historical Society* 36: 45–68.

(1992). *Charles the Bald*. London: Longman.

(1994). 'England and the Continent in the Anglo-Saxon Period'. In Nigel Saul, ed., *England in Europe, 1066–1453*. London: Collins and Brown: 21–35.

(1999). *Rulers and Ruling Families in Early Medieval Europe: Alfred, Charles the Bald, and Others*. Aldershot: Ashgate.

(2002). 'England and the Continent in the Ninth Century, I: Ends and Beginnings'. *Transactions of the Royal Historical Society* 12: 1–21.

(2015). 'Charlemagne and Europe'. *Journal of the British Academy* 2: 125–52.

(2019). *King and Emperor: A New Life of Charlemagne*. London: Allen Lane.

Netzer, Nancy (1994). *Cultural Interplay in the Eighth Century: The Trier Gospels and the Making of a Scriptorium at Echternach*. Cambridge: Cambridge University Press.

Nightingale, John (1996). 'Oswald, Fleury and Continental Reform'. In Nicholas Brooks and Catherine Cubitt, eds., *St Oswald of Worcester: Life and Influence.* London: Leicester University Press: 23–45.

Niles, John D. (2015). *The Idea of Anglo-Saxon England 1066–1901: Remembering, Forgetting, Deciphering, and Renewing the Past.* Chichester: Wiley Blackwell.

Noble, Thomas F. X. (2014). 'The Rise and Fall of the Archbishopric of Lichfield in English, Papal, and European Perspective'. In Francesca Tinti, ed., *England and Rome in the Early Middle Ages: Pilgrimage, Art and Politics.* Turnhout: Brepols, 291–305.

Ó Carragáin, Éamonn and Alan Thacker (2013). 'Wilfrid in Rome'. In N. J. Higham, ed., *Wilfrid: Abbot, Bishop, Saint. Papers from the 1300th Anniversary Conference.* Donnington: Shaun Tyas, 212–30.

Ortenberg, Veronica (1990). 'Archbishop Sigeric's Journey to Rome in 990'. *Anglo-Saxon England* 19: 197–246.

　(1992). *The English Church and the Continent in the Tenth and Eleventh Centuries: Cultural, Spiritual, and Artistic Exchanges.* Oxford: Oxford University Press.

　(2010). '"The King from Overseas": Why Did Æthelstan Matter in Tenth-Century Continental Affairs?' In David Rollason, Conrad Leyser and Hannah Williams, eds., *England and the Continent in the Tenth Century: Studies in Honour of Wilhelm Levison (1876–1947).* Turnhout: Brepols, 211–36.

Oschema, K. (2012). 'Medieval Europe – Object and Ideology'. In Teresa Pinheiro, Beata Cieszynska and José Eduardo Franco, eds., *Ideas of / for Europe.* Frankfurt: Peter Lang, 59–73.

Owen-Crocker, Gale R. (2004). *Dress in Anglo-Saxon England.* 2nd ed. Woodbridge: Boydell.

　(2005). 'Pomp, Piety, and Keeping the Woman in her Place: The Dress of Cnut and Ælfgifu-Emma'. *Medieval Clothing and Textiles* 1: 41–52.

Palmer, James T. (2009). *Anglo-Saxons in a Frankish World 690–900.* Turnhout: Brepols.

Pennington, Kenneth (1984). *Popes and Bishops: The Papal Monarchy in the Twelfth and Thirteenth Centuries.* Philadelphia: University of Pennsylvania Press.

Pelteret, David A. E. (1995). *Slavery in Early Medieval England: From the Reign of Alfred until the Twelfth Century.* Woodbridge: Boydell.

　(2011). 'Travel between England and Italy in the Early Middle Ages'. In Hans Sauer and Joanna Story with Gaby Waxenberger, eds., *Anglo-Saxon England and the Continent.* Tempe, AZ: ACMRS, 245–74.

(2014). 'Not All Roads Lead to Rome'. In Francesca Tinti, ed., *England and Rome in the Early Middle Ages: Pilgrimage, Art and Politics*. Turnhout: Brepols, 17–41.

Pohl, Walter (1997). 'Ethnic Names and Identities in the British Isles: A Comparative Perspective'. In John Hines, ed., *The Anglo-Saxons from the Migration Period to the Eighth Century: An Ethnographic Perspective*. Woodbridge: Boydell, 7–25.

Raaijmakers, Janneke (2012). *The Making of the Monastic Community of Fulda, c.774–c.900*. Cambridge: Cambridge University Press.

Rabin, Andrew (2010). 'Felix Liebermann and *Die Gesetze der Angelsachsen*'. In Stefan Jurasinski, Lisi Oliver and Andrew Rabin, eds., *English Law Before Magna Charta: Felix Liebermann and Die Gesetze der Angelsachsen*. Leiden: Brill, 1–8.

Rambaran-Olm, Mary (2019). 'Misnaming the Medieval: Rejecting "Anglo-Saxon" Studies'. *History Workshop*. www.historyworkshop.org.uk/mis naming-the-medieval-rejecting-anglo-saxon-studies/.

Reuter, Timothy (1998). 'The Making of England and Germany, 850–1050: Points of Comparison and Difference'. In Alfred P. Smyth, ed., *Medieval Europeans: Studies in Ethnic Identity and National Perspectives in Medieval Europe*. Basingstoke: Macmillan Press, 53–70.

Reynolds, Susan (1985). 'What Do We Mean by "Anglo-Saxon" and "Anglo-Saxons"?' *Journal of British Studies* 24: 395–414.

Richards, Julian D. and Dave Haldenby (2018). 'The Scale and Impact of Viking Settlement in Northumbria'. *Medieval Archaeology* 62: 322–50.

Ryan, Martin J. (2011). 'Place-Names, Languages and the Anglo-Saxon Landscape: An Introduction'. In Nicholas J. Higham and Martin J. Ryan, eds., *Place-Names, Languages and the Anglo-Saxon Landscape*. Woodbridge: Boydell, 1–21.

Santangeli Valenzani, Riccardo (2014). 'Hosting Foreigners in Early Medieval Rome: From *xenodochia* to *scholae peregrinorum*'. In Francesca Tinti, ed., *England and Rome in the Early Middle Ages: Pilgrimage, Art and Politics*. Turnhout: Brepols, 69–88.

Sawyer, Peter (1968). *Anglo-Saxon Charters: An Annotated List and Bibliography*. London: Royal Historical Society. Available in updated electronic format at https://esawyer.lib.cam.ac.uk/about/index.html.

Scharer, Anton (1996). 'The Writing of History at King Alfred's Court'. *Early Medieval Europe* 5: 177–206.

Schieffer, Rudolf (2000). 'Charlemagne and Rome'. In Julia M. H. Smith (ed.), *Early Medieval Rome and the Christian West: Essays in Honour of Donald A. Bullough*. Leiden: Brill, 279–95.

(2020). 'Boniface: His Life and Work'. In Michael Aaij and Shannon Godlove, eds., *A Companion to Boniface*. Leiden: Brill, 9–26.

Schieffer, Theodor (1954). *Winfrid-Bonifatius und die Christliche Grundlegung Europas*. Freiburg: Herder.

Schneidmüller, Bernd (1997). 'Die mittelalterlichen Konstruktionen Europas. Konvergenz und Differenzierung'. In Heinz Duchhardt and Andreas Kunz, eds., *'Europäische Geschichte' als historiographisches Problem*. Mainz: Philipp von Zabern, 5–24.

Schoenig, Steven A. (2016). *Bonds of Wool: The Pallium and Papal Power in the Middle Ages*. Washington, DC: Catholic University of America Press.

Smart, Veronica (1986). 'Scandinavians, Celts and Germans in Anglo-Saxon England: The Evidence of Moneyers' Names'. In Mark A. S. Blackburn, ed., *Anglo-Saxon Monetary History: Essays in Memory of Michael Dolley*. Leicester: Leicester University Press, 171–84.

Stafford, Pauline (1981). 'Charles the Bald, Judith and England'. In Margaret Gibson and Janet L. Nelson with David Ganz, eds., *Charles the Bald: Court and Kingdom. Papers Based on a Colloquium Held in London in April 1979*. Oxford: BAR, 137–51.

(1983). *Queens, Concubines and Dowagers: The King's Wife in the Early Middle Ages*. London: Leicester University Press.

(1997). *Queen Emma and Queen Edith: Queenship and Women's Power in Eleventh-Century England*. Oxford: Blackwell.

Stancliffe, Clare (1999). 'The British Church and the Mission of Augustine'. In Richard Gameson, ed., *St Augustine and the Conversion of England*. Stroud: Sutton Publishing, 107–51.

(2003). *Bede, Wilfrid, and the Irish*. Jarrow Lecture. Jarrow: St Paul's Church.

Story, Joanna (2003). *Carolingian Connections: Anglo-Saxon England and Carolingian Francia, c. 750–870*. Aldershot: Ashgate.

(2005). 'Charlemagne and the Anglo-Saxons'. In Joanna Story, ed., *Charlemagne: Empire and Society*. Manchester: Manchester University Press, 195–210.

(2012). 'Bede, Willibrord and the Letters of Pope Honorius I on the Genesis of the Archbishopric of York'. *The English Historical Review* 127: 783–818.

Thacker, Alan (1983). 'Bede's Ideal of Reform'. In Patrick Wormald with Donald Bullough and Roger Collins, eds., *Ideal and Reality in Frankish and Anglo-Saxon Society: Studies Presented to J. M. Wallace-Hadrill*. Oxford: Blackwell, 130–53.

(2008). 'Gallic or Greek? Archbishops in England from Theodore to Ecgberht'. In Paul Fouracre and David Ganz, eds., *Frankland: The Franks and the*

World of the Early Middle Ages. Essays in Honour of Dame Jinty Nelson. Manchester: Manchester University Press, 44–69.

Thomas, Rebecca (2020). 'Three Welsh Kings and Rome: Royal Pilgrimage, Overlordship, and Anglo-Welsh Relations in the Early Middle Ages'. *Early Medieval Europe* 28: 560–91.

Tinti, Francesca (2010). *Sustaining Belief: The Church of Worcester from c.870 to c.1100.* Farnham: Ashgate.

(2014). 'The Archiepiscopal Pallium in Late Anglo-Saxon England'. In Francesca Tinti, ed., *England and Rome in the Early Middle Ages: Pilgrimage, Art and Politics.* Turnhout: Brepols, 307–42.

(2015). 'Benedictine Reform and Pastoral Care in Late Anglo-Saxon England'. *Early Medieval Europe* 23: 229–51.

(2019). 'The Pallium Privilege of Pope Nicholas II for Archbishop Ealdred of York'. *The Journal of Ecclesiastical History* 70: 708–30.

(2020). 'The English Presence in Rome in the Later Anglo-Saxon Period: Change or Continuity?' In Scott DeGregorio and Paul Kershaw, eds., *Cities, Saints, and Communities in Early Medieval Europe: Essays in Honour of Alan Thacker.* Turnhout: Brepols, 345–71.

(2021). 'Anglo-Saxon Travellers and Their Books'. In Claire Breay and Joanna Story, eds., *Manuscripts in the Anglo-Saxon Kingdoms: Cultures and Connections.* Dublin: Four Courts Press, 168–77.

Townend, Matthew (2001). 'Contextualizing the *Knútsdrápur*: Skaldic Praise-Poetry at the Court of Cnut'. *Anglo-Saxon England* 30: 145–79.

(2002). *Language and History in Viking Age England: Linguistic Relations between Speakers of Old Norse and Old English.* Turnhout: Brepols.

(2011). 'Cnut's Poets: An Old Norse Literary Community in Eleventh-Century England'. In Elizabeth M. Tyler, ed., *Conceptualizing Multilingualism in England, c. 800–c. 1250.* Turnhout: Brepols, 197–215.

Treharne, Elaine (2012). *Living through Conquest: The Politics of Early English, 1020–1200.* Oxford: Oxford University Press.

(2014). 'The Performance of Piety: Cnut, Rome, and England'. In Francesca Tinti, ed., *England and Rome in the Early Middle Ages: Pilgrimage, Art and Politics.* Turnhout: Brepols, 343–64.

Tyler, Elizabeth M. (2011). 'Crossing Conquests: Polyglot Royal Women and Literary Culture in Eleventh-Century England'. In Elizabeth M. Tyler, ed., *Conceptualizing Multilingualism in England, c. 800–c. 1250.* Turnhout: Brepols, 171–96.

(2017). *England in Europe: English Royal Women and Literary Patronage, c. 1000–c. 1150.* Toronto: Toronto University Press.

Vanderputten, Steven (2006). 'Canterbury and Flanders in the Late Tenth Century'. *Anglo-Saxon England* 35: 219–44.

Wallace-Hadrill, J. M. (1950). 'The Franks and the English in the Ninth Century: Some Common Historical Interests'. *History* 35: 202–18.

(1960). 'Rome and the Early English Church: Some Questions of Transmission'. *Settimane del Centro italiano di studi sull'alto Medioevo* 7: 519–48.

(1962). *Bede's Europe*. Jarrow Lecture. Jarrow: St Paul's Church.

(1971). *Early Germanic Kingship in England and on the Continent: The Ford Lectures delivered in the University of Oxford in Hilary Term 1970*. Oxford: Clarendon Press.

Weaver, Erica (2018). 'Finding Consolation at the End of the Millennium'. In A. Joseph McMullen and Erica Weaver, eds., *The Legacy of Boethius in Medieval England: The Consolation and its Afterlife*. Tempe, AZ: ACMRS, 89–102.

West, Charles (2015). 'England: Apart from or a Part of Europe? An Early Medieval Perspective'. *History Matters: History Brought Alive by the University of Sheffield*, 14 May. www.historymatters.group.shef.ac.uk/eng land-part-europe-early-medieval-perspective/.

(2019). 'Plenty of Puff'. *London Review of Books* 41(24), 19 December. www.lrb.co.uk/the-paper/v41/n24/charles-west/plenty-of-puff.

Wieland, Gernot (1991). 'Anglo-Saxon Culture in Bavaria 739–850'. *Mediaevalia* 17: 177–200.

Williams, Ann (1986). '"Cockles amongst the Wheat": Danes and English in the Western Midlands in the First Half of the Eleventh Century'. *Midland History* 11: 1–22.

Wilton, David (2020). 'What Do We Mean by *Anglo-Saxon*? Pre-Conquest to the Present'. *Journal of English and Germanic Philology* 119: 425–56.

Wood, Ian (1983). *The Merovingian North Sea*. Alingsås: Viktoria Bokförlag.

(1999). 'Augustine and Gaul'. In Richard Gameson, ed., *St Augustine and the Conversion of England*. Stroud: Sutton Publishing: 68–82.

(2001). *The Missionary Life: Saints and the Evangelisation of Europe 400 – 1050*. Harlow: Longman.

(2004). 'John Michael Wallace-Hadrill, 1916–1985'. *Proceedings of the British Academy* 124: 333–55.

(2011). 'The Continental Connections of Anglo-Saxon Courts from Æthelberht to Offa', *Settimane del Centro italiano di studi sull'alto Medioevo* 58: 443–80.

(2013). 'The Continental Journeys of Wilfrid and Biscop'. In N. J. Higham, ed., *Wilfrid: Abbot, Bishop, Saint. Papers from the 1300th Anniversary Conference*. Donnington: Shaun Tyas, 200–11.

Wood, Michael (1983). 'The Making of King Æthelstan's Empire: An English Charlemagne?' In Patrick Wormald with Donald Bullough and Roger Collins, eds., *Ideal and Reality in Frankish and Anglo-Saxon Society: Studies Presented to J. M. Wallace-Hadrill*. Oxford: Blackwell, 250–72.

(2014). 'A Carolingian Scholar in the Court of King Æthelstan'. In David Rollason, Conrad Leyser and Hannah Williams, eds., *England and the Continent in the Tenth Century: Studies in Honour of Wilhelm Levison (1876–1947)*. Turnhout: Brepols, 135–62.

(2019). 'As a Racism Row Rumbles on, Is it Time to Retire the Term "Anglo-Saxon"?' *BBC History Magazine*, December. www.historyextra.com /period/anglo-saxon/professor-michael-wood-anglo-saxon-name-debate-is-term-racist/.

Wormald, Patrick (1988). 'Æthelwold and His Continental Counterparts: Contact, Comparison, Contrast'. In Barbara Yorke, ed., *Bishop Æthelwold: His Career and Influence*. Woodbridge: Boydell, 13–42. Reprinted in Patrick Wormald (2006). *The Times of Bede: Studies in Early English Christian Society and its Historian*, ed. Stephen Baxter. Malden, MA: Blackwell: no. 5.

(1992). 'The Venerable Bede and the "Church of the English"'. In Geoffrey Rowell, ed., *The English Tradition and the Genius of Anglicanism: Studies in Commemoration of the Second Centenary of John Keble*. Wantage: Ikon Productions, 13–32. Reprinted in Wormald, Patrick (2006) *The Times of Bede: Studies in Early English Christian Society and Its Historian*, ed. Stephen Baxter. Malden, MA: Blackwell: no. 6.

Wright, Roger (2002). *A Sociophilological Study of Late Latin*. Turnhout: Brepols.

(2011). 'Abbo of Fleury in Ramsey (985–987)'. In Elizabeth M. Tyler, ed., *Conceptualizing Multilingualism in England, c. 800–c. 1250*. Turnhout: Brepols, 105–120.

Yorke, Barbara (2006). *The Conversion of Britain: Religion, Politics and Society in Britain c.600–800*. Harlow: Pearson Longman.

(2020) 'Bede's Preferential Treatment of the Irish'. In Scott DeGregorio and Paul Kershaw, eds., *Cities, Saints, and Communities in Early Medieval Europe: Essays in Honour of Alan Thacker*. Turnhout: Brepols, 223–40.

(2020). 'Boniface's West Saxon Background'. In Michael Aaij and Shannon Godlove, eds., *A Companion to Boniface*. Leiden: Brill, 27–45.

Zacher, Samantha (2011). 'Multilingualism at the Court of King Æthelstan: Latin Praise Poetry and *The Battle of Brunanburh*'. In Elizabeth M. Tyler, ed., *Conceptualizing Multilingualism in England, c. 800–c. 1250*. Turnhout: Brepols, 77–103.

Acknowledgements

I would like to thank Megan Cavell, Rory Naismith, Winfried Rudolf and Emily Thornbury for inviting me to contribute to the Elements in England in the Early Medieval World series. I am also grateful to the several friends and colleagues who have provided much valuable help through discussion on specific points as well as access to unpublished work: Lesley Abrams, Helen Appleton, Claire Breay, Caitlin Ellis, Simon Keynes, Ryan Lavelle, Jinty Nelson, Steffen Patzold, Christine Rauer, Levi Roach, Jo Story, Erica Weaver and Charles West. My deepest thanks are due to Robert Gallagher, Rory Naismith, Edward Roberts and the peer reviewers for reading a previous draft of this Element and making several helpful suggestions. Any remaining errors are my own responsibility. This publication is for Luis, my husband, and Emma, our daughter; their presence in my life is the best outcome of my 'European connections'.

Cambridge Elements $\equiv$

England in the Early Medieval World

Megan Cavell
University of Birmingham

Megan Cavell is a Birmingham Fellow in medieval English literature at the University of Birmingham. She works on a wide range of topics in medieval literary studies, from Old and early Middle English and Latin languages and literature to gender, material culture and animal studies. Her previous publications include *Weaving Words and Binding Bodies: The Poetics of Human Experience in Old English Literature* (2016), and she is co-editor of *Riddles at Work in the Anglo-Saxon Tradition: Words, Ideas, Interactions* with Jennifer Neville (forthcoming).

Rory Naismith
University of Cambridge

Rory Naismith is Lecturer in the History of England Before the Norman Conquest in the Department of Anglo-Saxon, Norse and Celtic at the University of Cambridge and a Fellow of Corpus Christi College, Cambridge. Also a Fellow of the Royal Historical Society, he is the author of *Citadel of the Saxons: The Rise of Early London* (2018), *Medieval European Coinage, with a Catalogue of the Coins in the Fitzwilliam Museum, Cambridge, 8: Britain and Ireland c. 400–1066* (2017) and *Money and Power in Anglo-Saxon England: The Southern English Kingdoms 757–865* (2012, which won the 2013 International Society of Anglo-Saxonists First Book Prize).

Winfried Rudolf
University of Göttingen

Winfried Rudolf is Chair of Medieval English Language and Literature in the University of Göttingen (Germany). Recent publications include *Childhood and Adolescence in Anglo-Saxon Literary Culture* with Susan E. Irvine (2018). He has published widely on Anglo-Saxon homiletic literature and is currently principal investigator of the ERC-Project ECHOE–Electronic Corpus of Anonymous Homilies in Old English.

Emily V. Thornbury
Yale University

Emily V. Thornbury is Associate Professor of English at Yale University. She studies the literature and art of early England, with a particular emphasis on English and Latin poetry. Her publications include *Becoming a Poet in Anglo-Saxon England* (2014), and, co-edited with Rebecca Stephenson, *Latinity and Identity in Anglo-Saxon Literature* (2016). She is currently working on a monograph called *The Virtue of Ornament*, about Anglo-Saxon theories of aesthetic value.

About the Series

Elements in England in the Early Medieval World takes an innovative, interdisciplinary view of the culture, history, literature, archaeology and legacy of England between the fifth and eleventh centuries. Individual contributions question and situate key themes, and thereby bring new perspectives to the heritage of Anglo-Saxon England. They draw on texts in Latin and Old English as well as material culture to paint a vivid picture of the period. Relevant not only to students and scholars working in medieval studies, these volumes explore the rich intellectual, methodological and comparative value that the dynamic researchers interested in the Anglo-Saxon World have to offer in a modern, global context. The series is driven by a commitment to inclusive and critical scholarship, and to the view that Anglo-Saxon studies have a part to play in many fields of academic research, as well as constituting a vibrant and self-contained area of research in its own right.

Cambridge Elements⁼

England in the Early Medieval World

Printed in the United States
by Baker & Taylor Publisher Services